Rainbow Edition

Reading Mastery I
Seatwork

Siegfried Engelmann • Elaine C. Bruner

Macmillan/McGraw-Hill
Columbus, Ohio

Note to the Teacher

The activities in this book reinforce the materials presented in the *Reading Mastery I* program. They correlate with *Reading Mastery* in their orthography, vocabulary, and skill development. If you are using the *Reading Mastery: Fast Cycle* program, a lesson conversion chart appears on the last page of this book.

Each activity focuses on a major reading skill in one of the following categories: sound discrimination, word recognition, sentence structure, literal comprehension, following directions, sequencing, inferential comprehension, and paraphrasing. The skill is identified at the bottom of each page.

The directions at the top of each page are to be read to the students. Most children will be able to work the activities without further help, but some children will need more guidance. You may want to expand on the directions and perhaps even "walk through" each new type of activity with your students the first time it appears. If your students appear to be having difficulty with a particular activity, just skip those activities for a while. You may want to try them again later, when you think your children are ready for them.

School Use of Blackline Masters

The blackline masters in this book can be used for making duplicating masters or for photocopying. They may be reproduced for classroom use by schools without the prior written permission of SRA.

ACKNOWLEDGMENTS

SRA wishes to acknowledge the contributions of Linda Olen, Jill Walsh, and Linda Zahorak in the development of these materials.

SRA Macmillan/McGraw-Hill
250 Old Wilson Bridge Road
Suite 310
Worthington, Ohio 43085
Printed in the United States of America.
ISBN 0-02-686416-9
3 4 5 6 7 8 9 0 PAT 99

Name ____________________ **Lesson 1**

This is a star. (*Point to the star in the upper left corner.*) Find the other stars hidden in this picture. Trace each star with red. Then color the rest of the picture. But don't use red for anything except the stars.

Name ______________________________ **Lesson 2**

Parts of this picture are missing. Find where the missing parts should be and draw them in. Then color the whole picture.

Name ______________________________ Lesson 3

Cut out the trees at the bottom of the page. Cut along the dotted lines. Paste each tree next to the one that looks just like it. Then color all the trees.

Name ____ **Lesson 4**

This is a triangle. (*Point to the triangle in the upper left corner.*) Find the other triangles hidden in this picture. Trace each triangle with red. Then color the rest of the picture. But don't use red for anything except the triangles.

Name ____

Parts of this picture are missing. Find where the missing parts should be and draw them in. Then color the whole picture.

Name ____________________ **Lesson 6**

Cut out the kites at the bottom of the page. Cut along the dotted lines. Paste each kite next to the one that looks just like it. Then color all the kites.

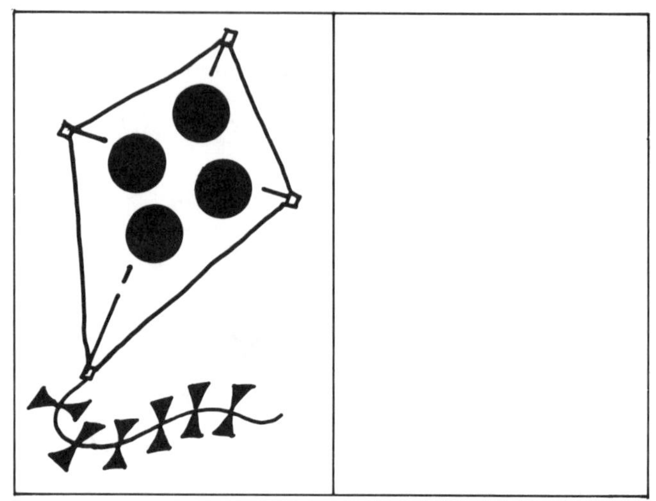
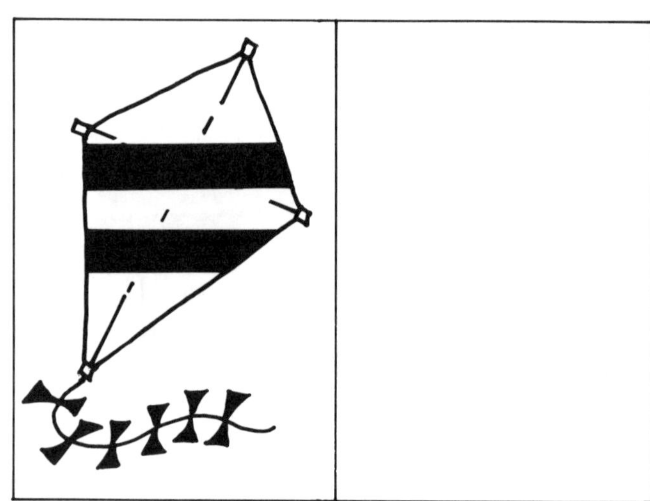
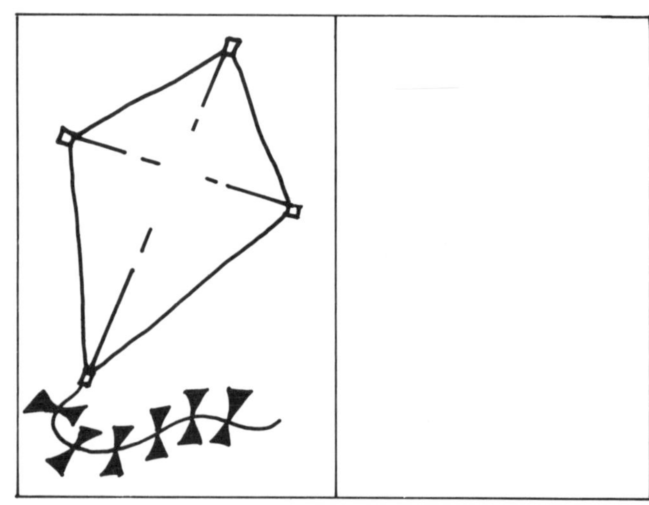
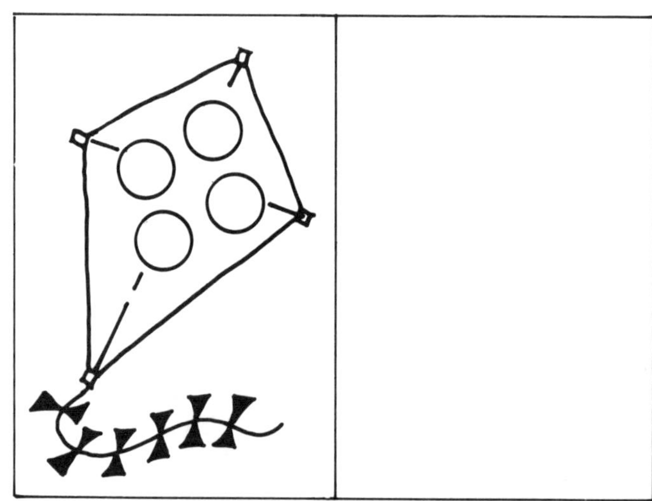
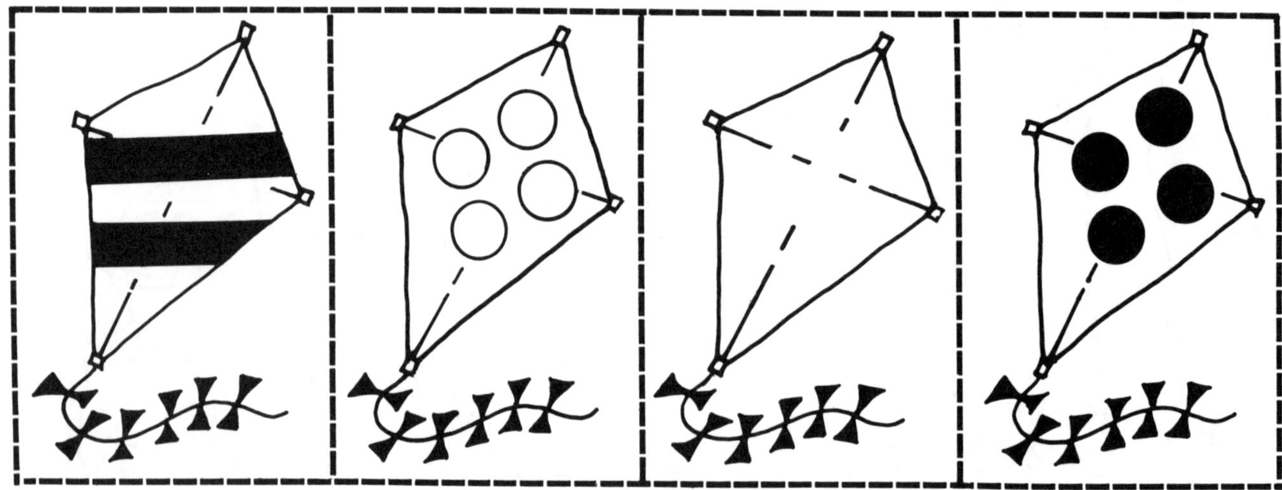

Name ____________________

Cut out the pictures at the bottom of the page. Cut along the dotted lines. Paste each picture under the one that is just like it. Then color all the pictures.

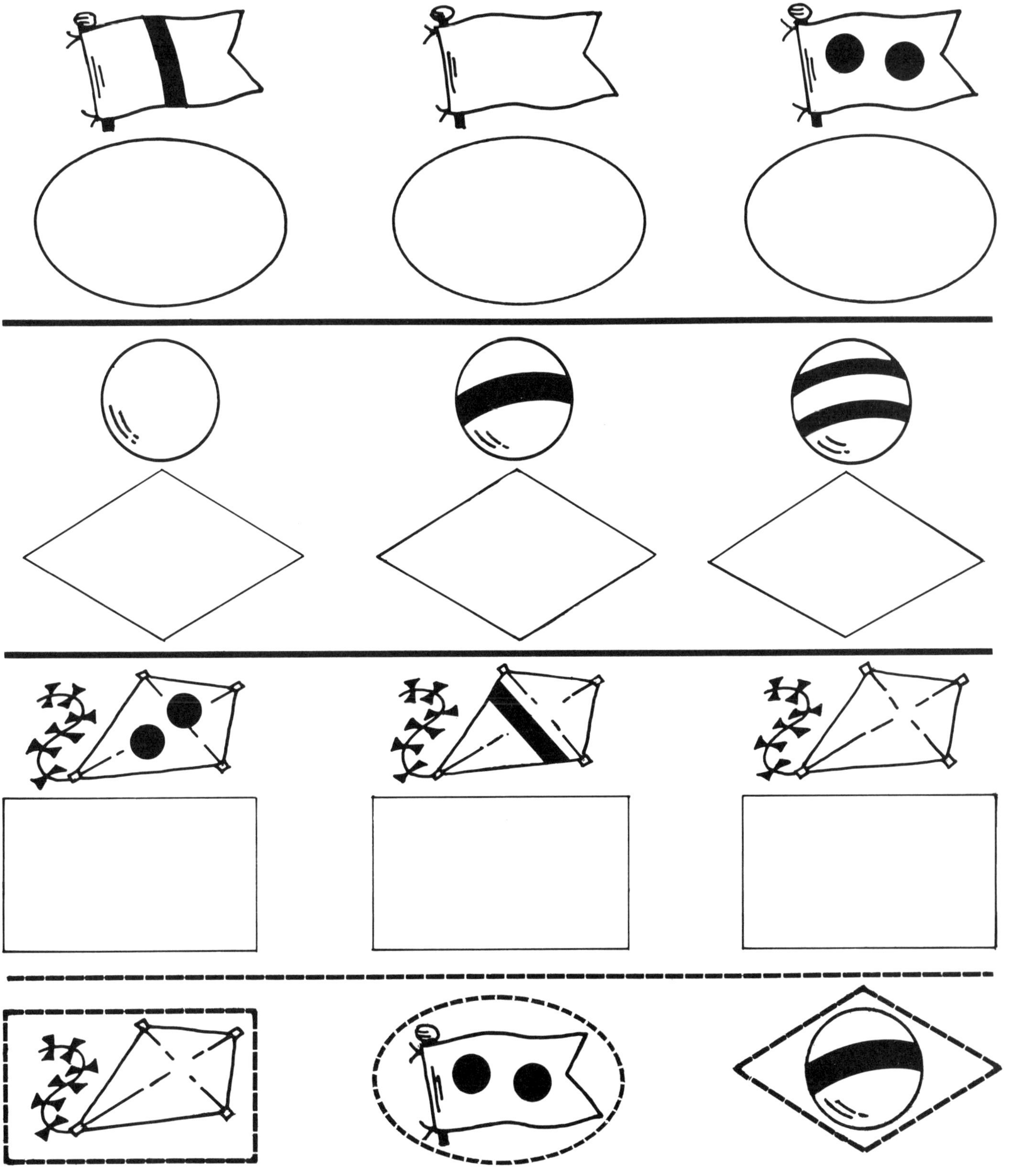

Name ____________________ Lesson 8

This is a circle. (*Point to the circle in the upper left corner.*) Find the other circles hidden in this picture. Trace each circle with red. Then color the rest of the picture. But don't use red for anything except the circles.

Name ______________________________

Cut out the pictures at the bottom of the page. Cut along the dotted lines. Paste each picture under the one that is just like it. Then color all the pictures.

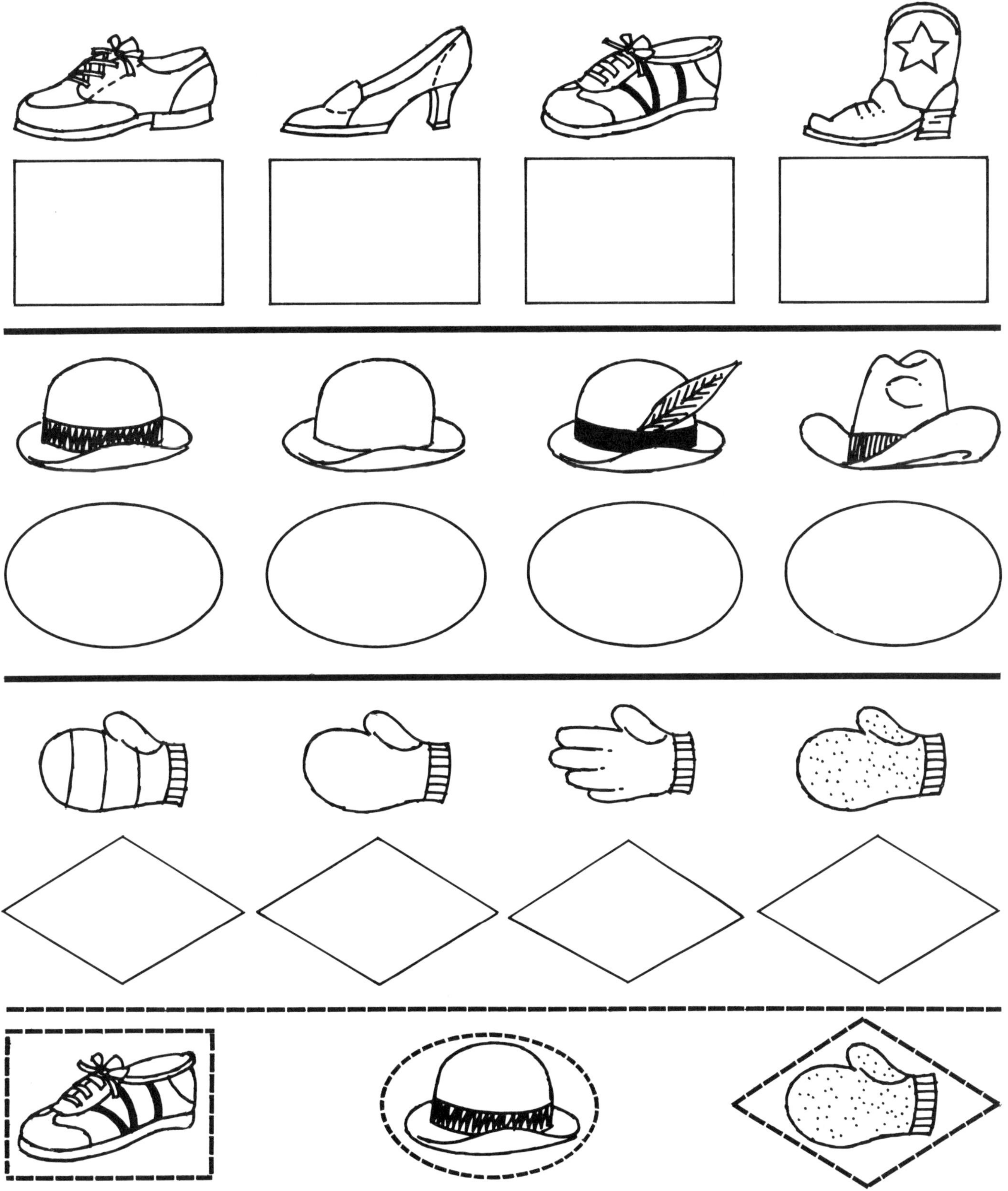

Name ____________________

Parts of this picture are missing. Find where the missing parts should be and draw them in. Then color the whole picture.

Name ____ **Lesson 11**

Cut out the pictures at the bottom of the page. Cut along the dotted lines. Paste each picture under the one that is just like it. Then color all the pictures.

Name ______________________________ **Lesson 12**

First trace the *mmm*'s on the page. Then start with the big *mmm* in the box and follow the dotted line from *mmm* to *mmm*. You'll make a picture of something that monkeys like to play in. Color the picture that you make.

Name ______________________________ Lesson 13

Help the alligator get to the river. Start with the alligator at the top of the puzzle and draw a line from *aaa* to *aaa* until you reach the river. When you finish, fill in the row of *aaa*'s at the bottom of the page.

a a a a a a a

Name ______________________________ Lesson 14

Trace the sounds at the bottom of the page. Then cut them out. Cut along the dotted lines. Paste the sounds on the matching sounds in the picture. When you finish, color the picture.

m a m a m a

Name ______________________________ Lesson 15

In each row, circle the picture that goes with the thing in the box. When you finish all the rows, draw something that goes with the dog at the bottom of the page. Color your picture.

Name ____ **Lesson 16**

Trace the sounds at the bottom of the page. Then cut them out. Cut along the dotted lines. Paste the sounds on the matching sounds in the picture. When you finish, color the picture.

a m a m a m

Name ______________________________

First trace the *sss*'s on the page. Then start with the big *sss* in the box and follow the dotted line from *sss* to *sss*. You'll make a picture of a big sailboat. Color the picture that you make.

Name ______________________________ Lesson 18

There's a picture hidden on this page. To find the hidden picture, color all the shapes that have *sss* in them brown.

Name ______________________________ **Lesson 19**

In each row, circle the picture that goes with the thing in the box. When you finish all the rows, draw something that goes with the monkey at the bottom of the page. Color your picture.

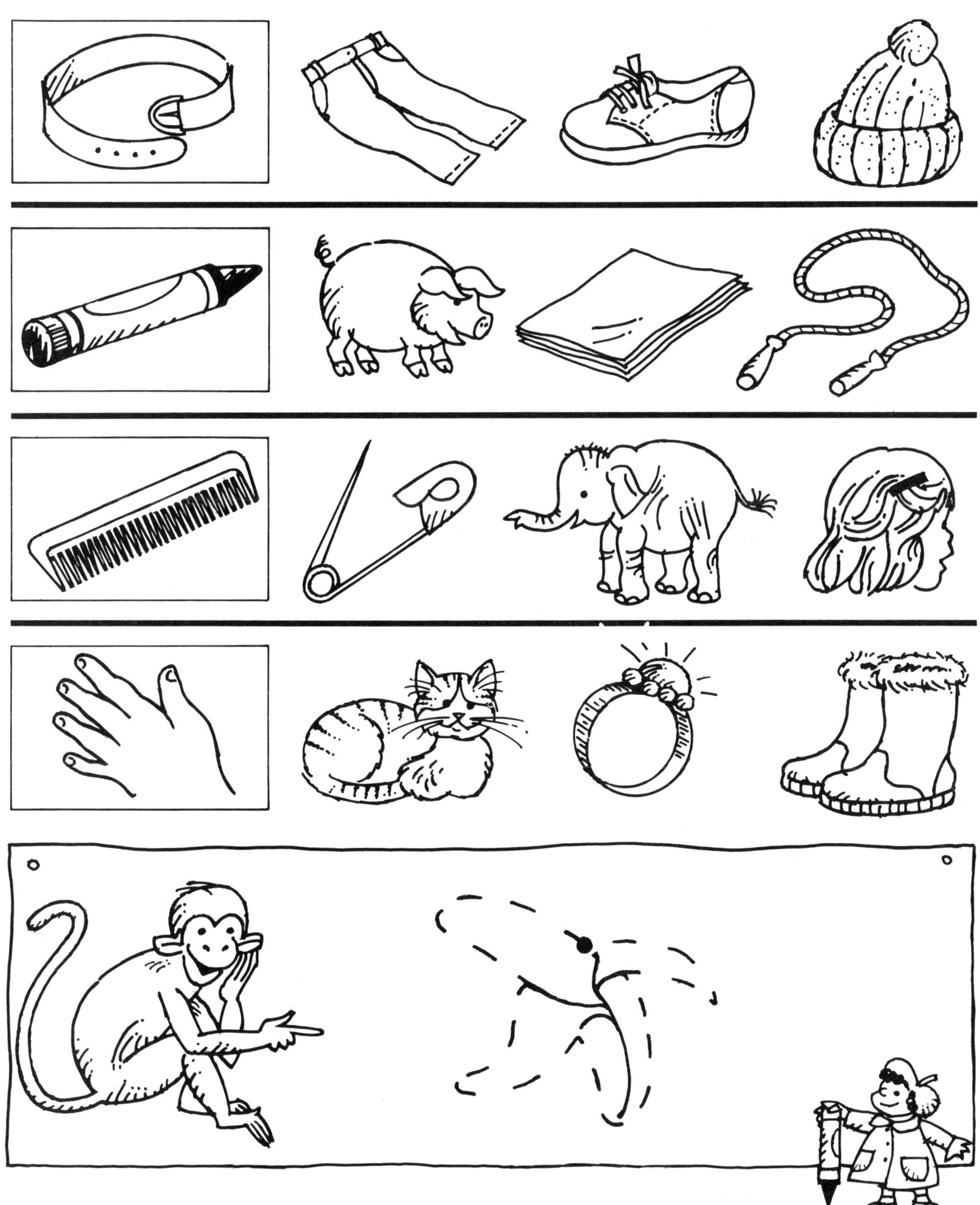

Name ______ ______________________________ **Lesson 20**

Help the eagle get to its nest. Start with the eagle at the bottom of the puzzle and draw a line from ēēē to ēēē until you reach the nest. When you finish, fill in the row of ēēē's at the bottom of the page.

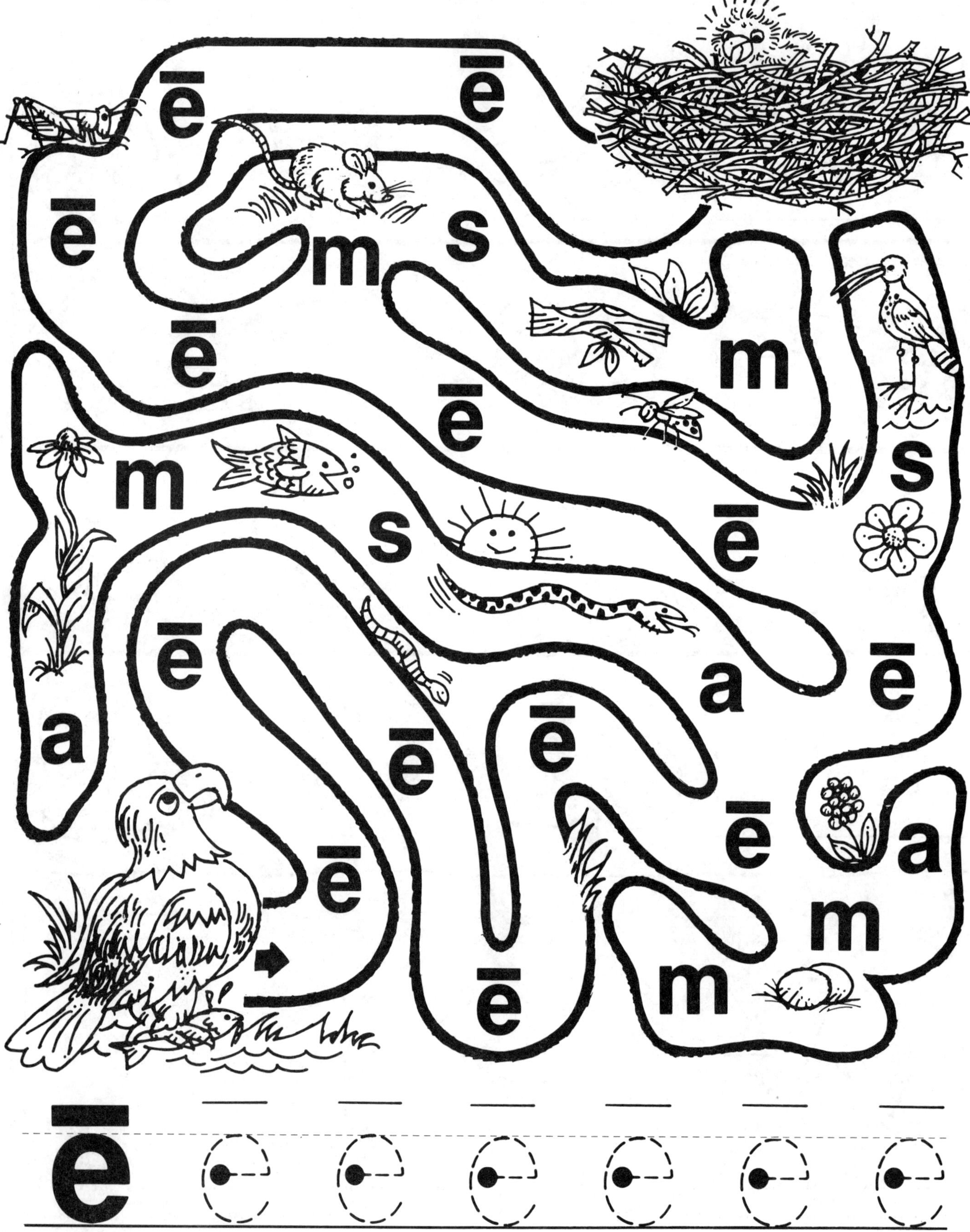

ē

Name ____ **Lesson 21**

There's a picture hidden on this page. To find the hidden picture, color all the shapes that have *ēēē* in them black.

Name ____ Lesson 22

In each row, circle the picture that goes with the thing in the box. When you finish all the rows, draw something that goes with the light bulb at the bottom of the page. Color your picture.

Name ____ **Lesson 23**

One of the pictures in each row is in a box. One of the other pictures in the row tells *why* the picture in the box happened. Circle the pictures that tell *why*. When you finish, color all the pictures.

Name ____ Lesson 24

Help the rocketship get to the moon. Start with the rocketship and draw a line from *rrr* to *rrr* until you reach the moon. When you finish, fill in the row of *rrr*'s at the bottom of the page.

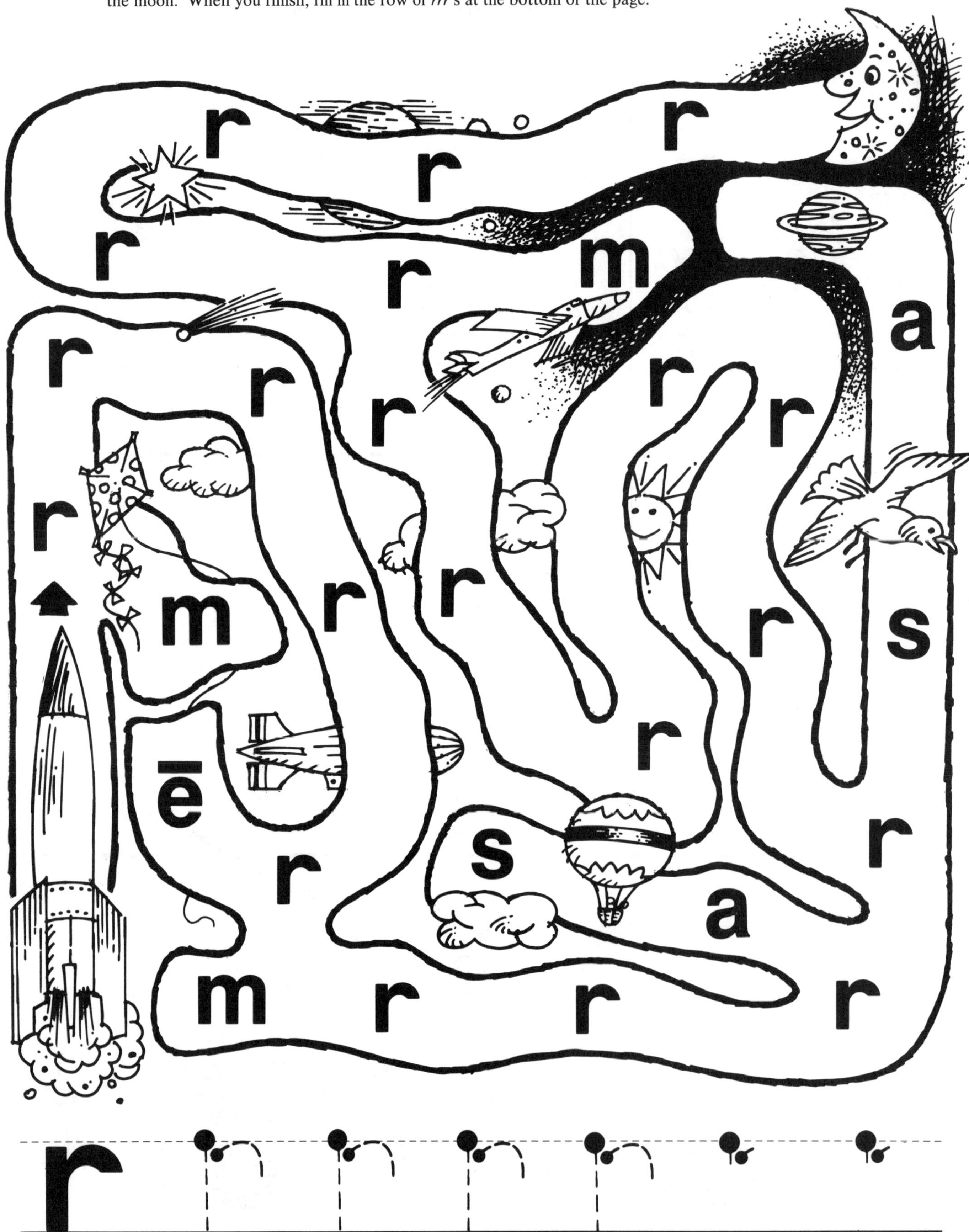

r

Name ____________________

There's an animal hidden on this page. To find the animal, cut out the boxes at the bottom of the page. Cut along the dotted lines. Paste each box on the one that has the same sound in it. Color the animal that you find.

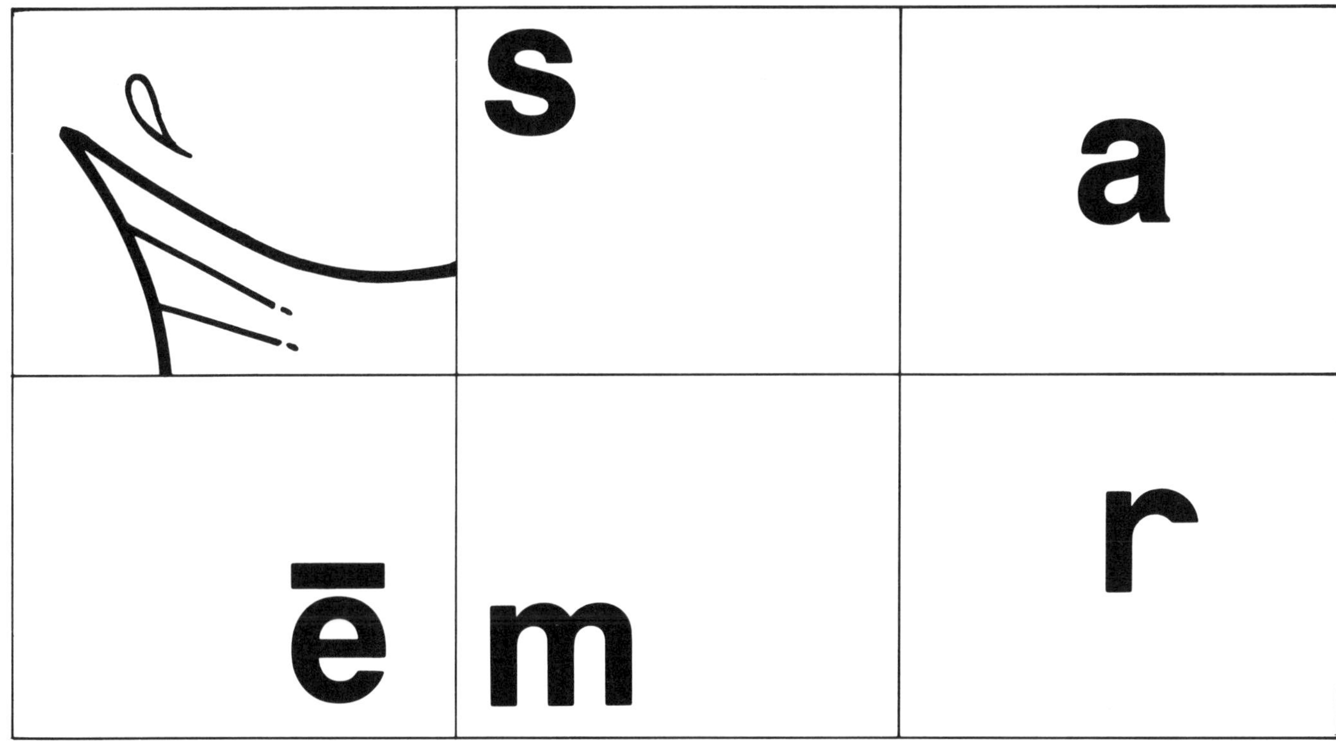

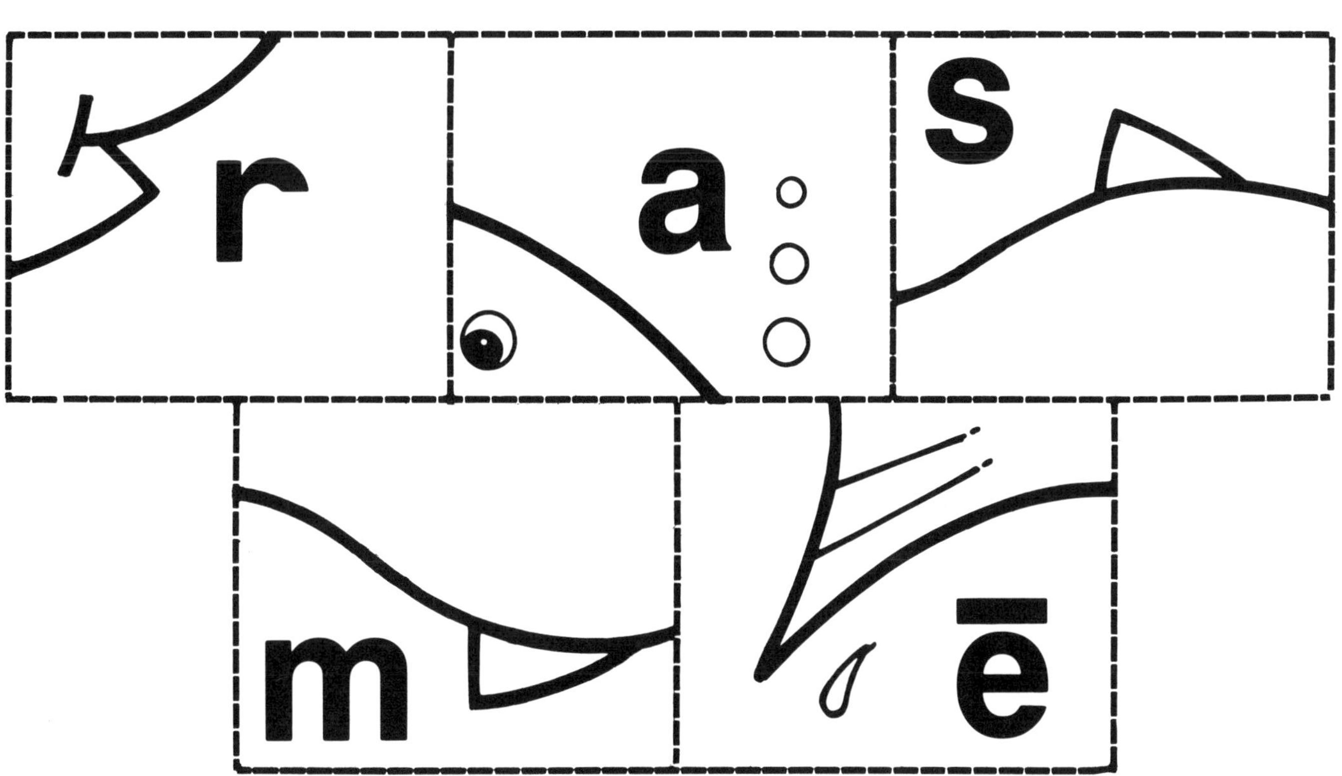

One of the pictures in each row is in a box. One of the other pictures in the row tells *why* the picture in the box happened. Circle the pictures that tell *why*. When you finish, color all the pictures.

In each row, circle the picture that goes with the thing in the box. When you finish all the rows, draw something that goes with the nest at the bottom of the page. Color your picture.

Name ____ **Lesson 28**

Find the *d*'s hidden in this picture. Trace each *d* with red. Then color the rest of the picture. But don't use red for anything except the *d*'s.

Name ______________________________ **Lesson 29**

There's an animal hidden on this page. To find the animal, cut out the boxes at the bottom of the page. Cut along the dotted lines. Paste each box on the one that has the same sound in it. Color the animal that you find.

d	ē	r
s	a	m

Name ______________________________ Lesson 30

One of the pictures in each row is in a box. One of the other pictures in the row tells *why* the picture in the box happened. Circle the pictures that tell *why*. When you finish, color all the pictures.

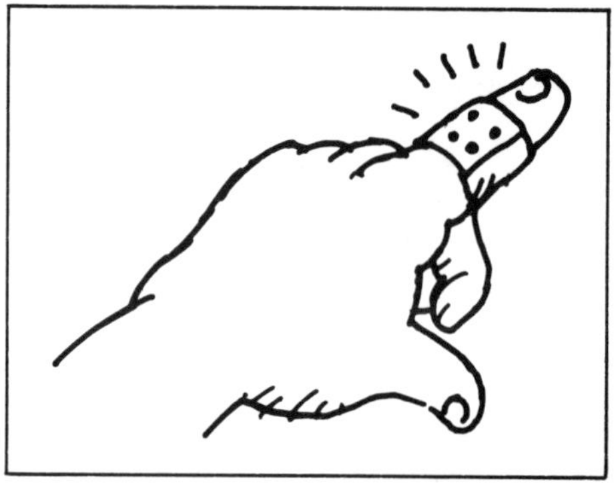

There's a picture hidden on this page. To find the hidden picture, color all the shapes that have *d* in them green.

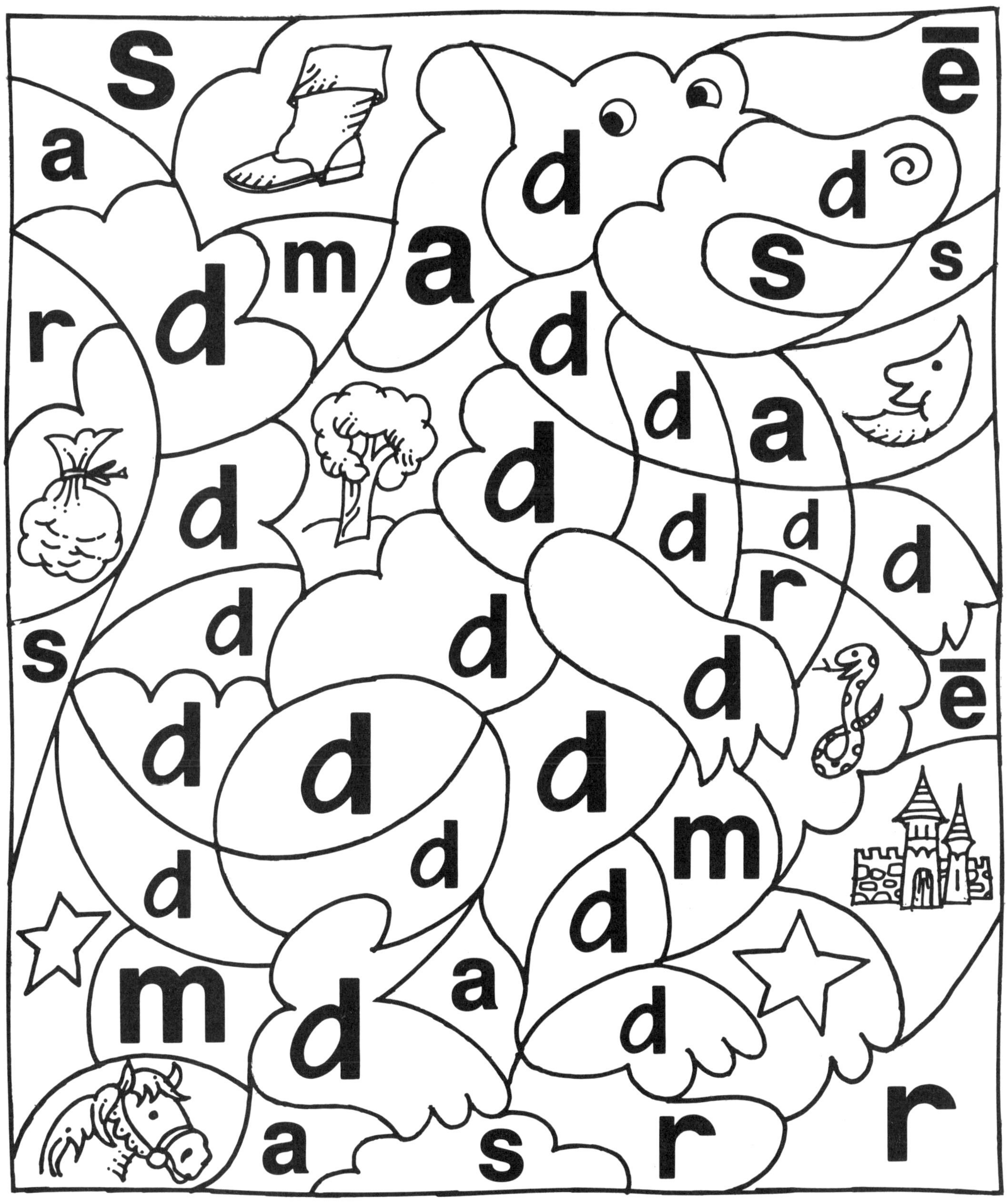

Name ____________________

Help the foot get to the shoe. Start with the foot at the top of the puzzle and draw a line from *fff* to *fff* until you reach the shoe. When you finish, fill in the row of *fff*'s at the bottom of the page.

f

There's an animal hidden on this page. To find the animal, cut out the boxes at the bottom of the page. Cut along the dotted lines. Paste each box on the one that has the same word in it. Color the animal that you find.

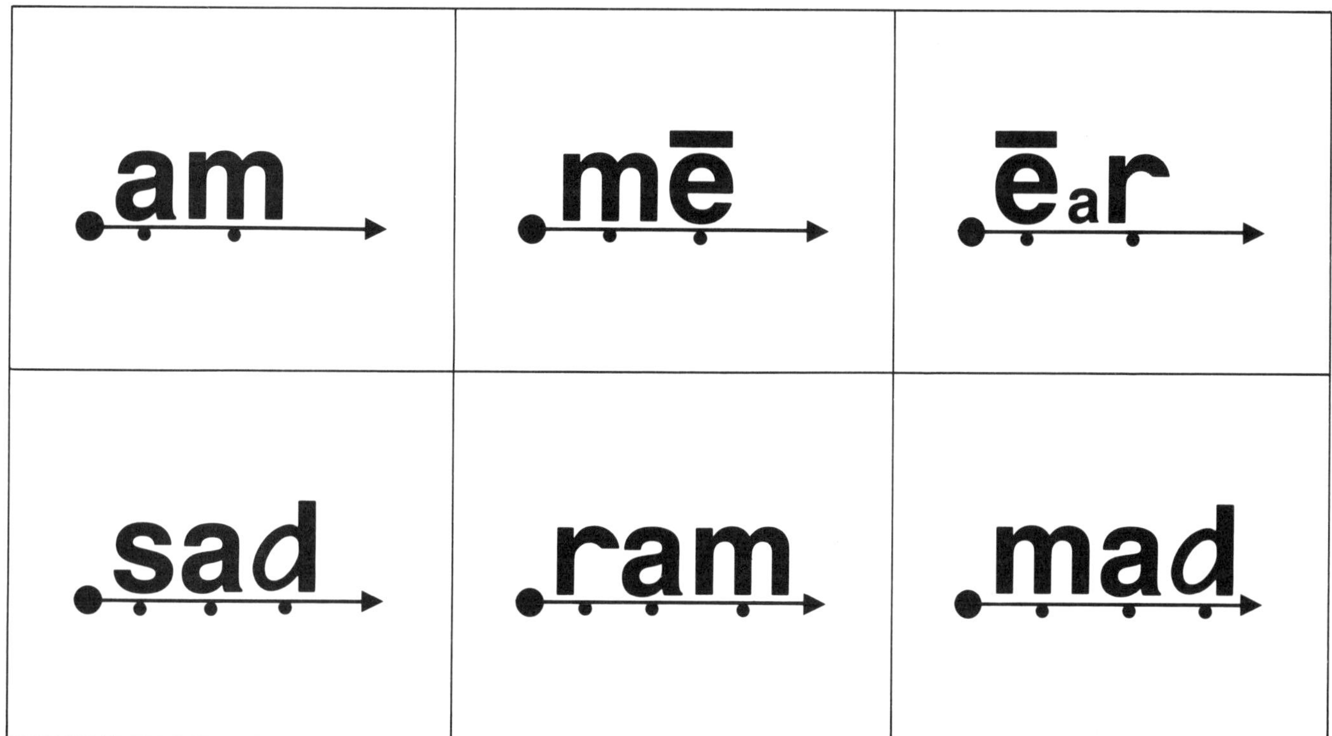

Name ______________________________ Lesson 34

One of the pictures in each row is in a box. One of the other pictures in the row tells *why* the picture in the box happened. Circle the pictures that tell *why*. When you finish, color all the pictures.

Name ____________________ Lesson 35

There's a picture hidden on this page. To find the hidden picture, color all the shapes that have *iii* in them orange.

Name ______________________________ **Lesson 36**

Put the pictures in order. In each row, put a *1* by the picture that happens *first* and a *2* by the picture that happens *next*. When you finish the page, go back and color the pictures.

Name ______________________________ Lesson 37

There's an animal hidden on this page. To find the animal, cut out the boxes at the bottom of the page. Cut along the dotted lines. Paste each box on the one that has the same word in it. Color the animal that you find.

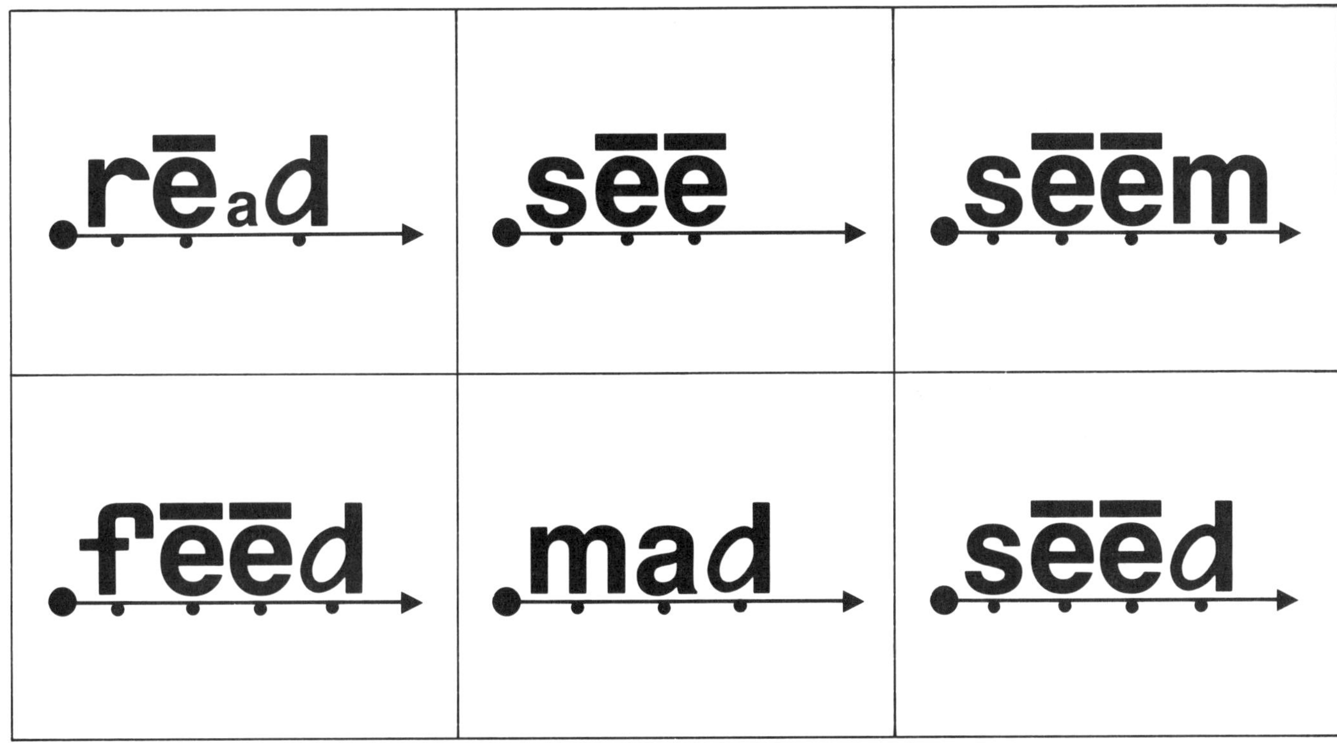

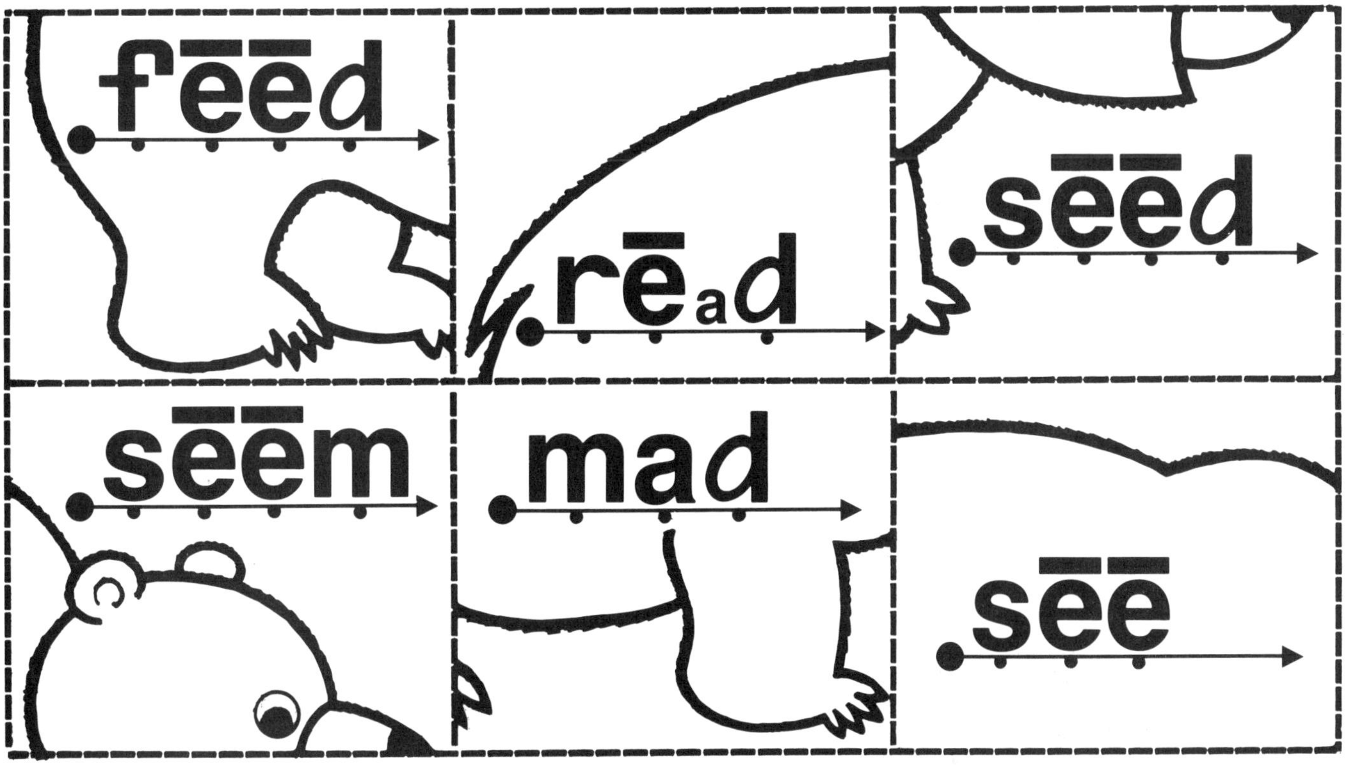

feed
read
seed
seem
mad
see

Name ____________________

Put the pictures in order. In each row, put a *1* by the picture that happens *first* and a *2* by the picture that happens *next*. When you finish the page, go back and color the pictures.

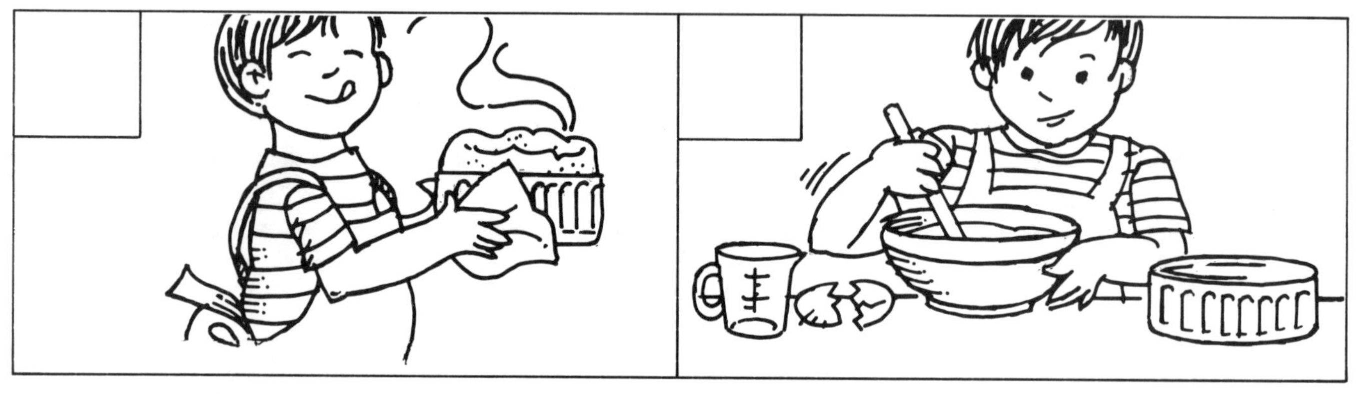

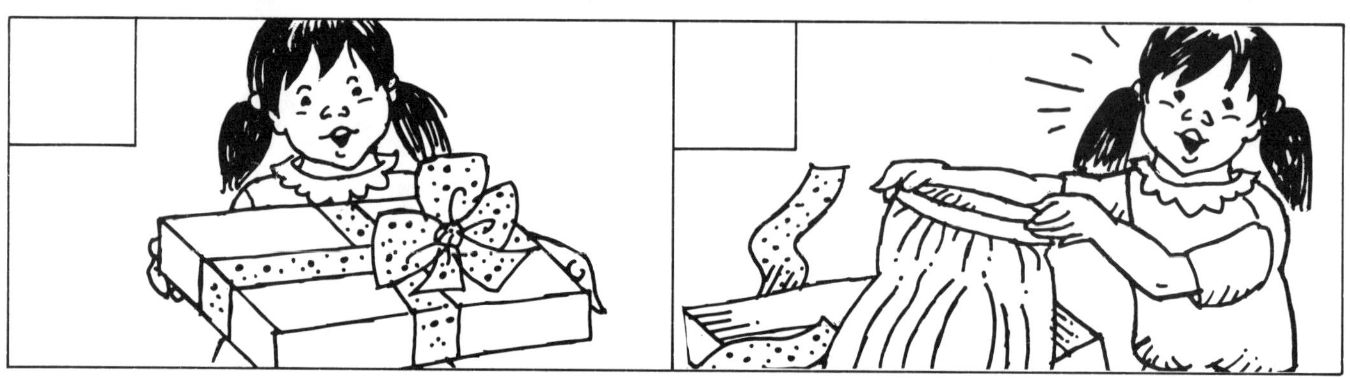

Name ______________________________ **Lesson 39**

Find the *ththth*'s hidden in this picture. Trace each *ththth* with red. Then color the rest of the picture. But don't use red for anything except the *ththth*'s.

Name ______________________________ Lesson 40

Write the words on the page. First trace each word. Then write the word two times by yourself. When you finish, draw a picture of somebody saying *me*.

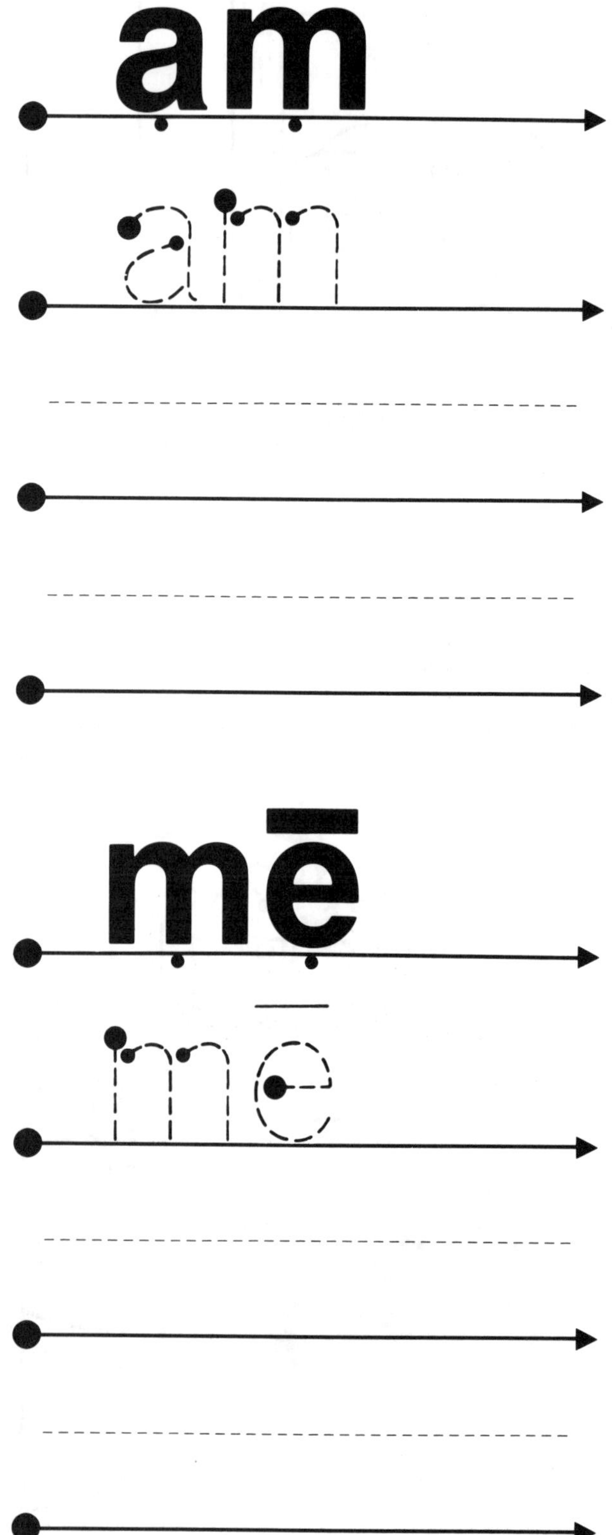

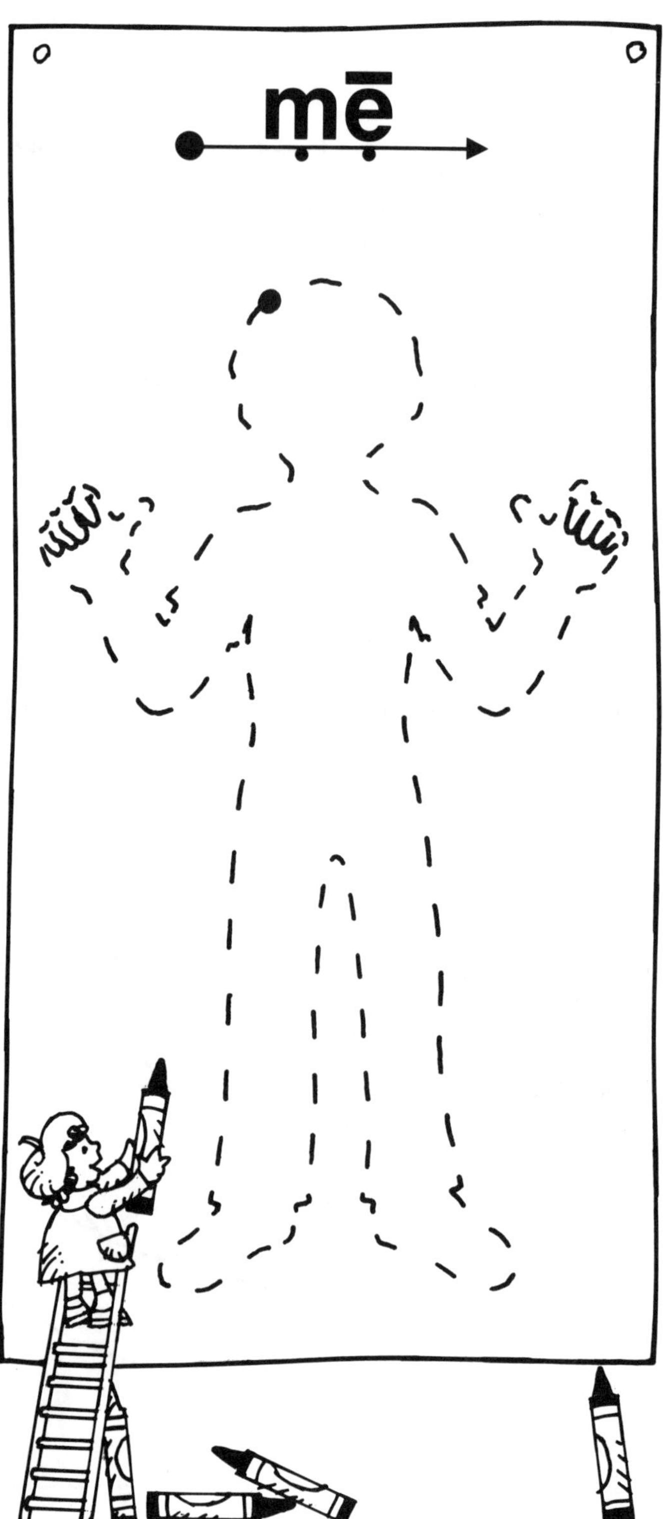

Name ____ Lesson 41

Put the pictures in order. In each row, put a *1* by the picture that happens *first* and a *2* by the picture that happens *next*. When you finish the page, go back and color the pictures.

Name ____________________ Lesson 42

Put the pictures in order. In each row, put a *1* by the picture that happens *first*, a *2* by the picture that happens *next*, and a *3* by the picture that happens *last*. When you finish the page, go back and color the pictures.

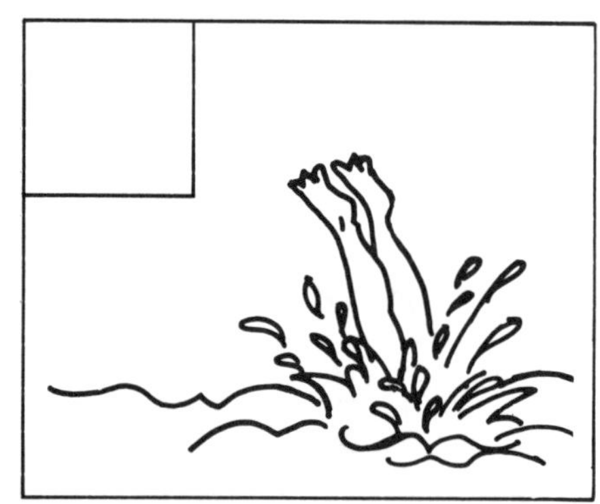

Put the pictures in order. In each row, put a *1* by the picture that happens *first*, a *2* by the picture that happens *next*, and a *3* by the picture that happens *last*. When you finish the page, go back and color the pictures.

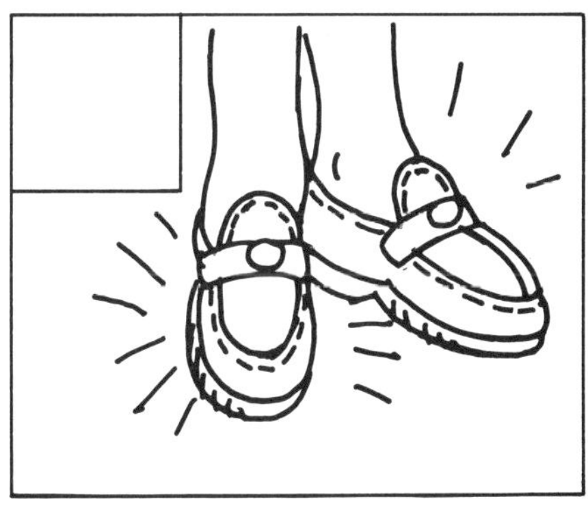
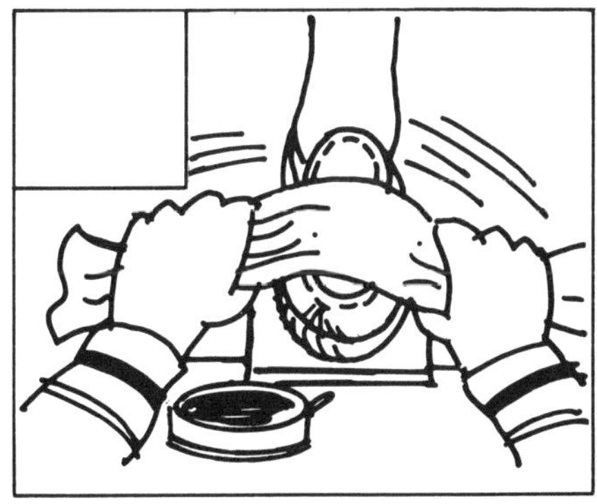
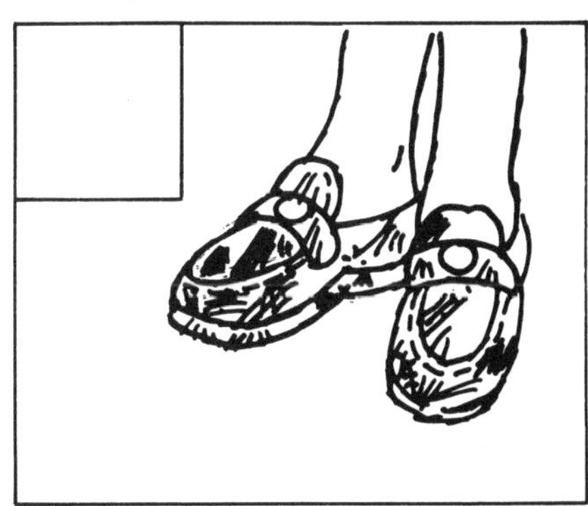

Name ____________________

Read the word on the arrow at the beginning of each row of letters. That word is hidden in the row of letters. Find the hidden words and circle them. Then draw a picture of an animal that is *sad*.

fēēd	f	d	f	ē	ē	d	ē	f
mad	a	m	d	m	d	m	a	d
mē	ē	m	m	ē	ē	ē	m	m
ram	m	r	a	r	a	m	m	a
am	m	m	a	a	a	m	m	a
sēē	ē	ē	s	ē	s	ē	ē	s
sēēd	d	s	ē	ē	d	ē	s	ē
sad	s	a	d	d	s	a	a	d

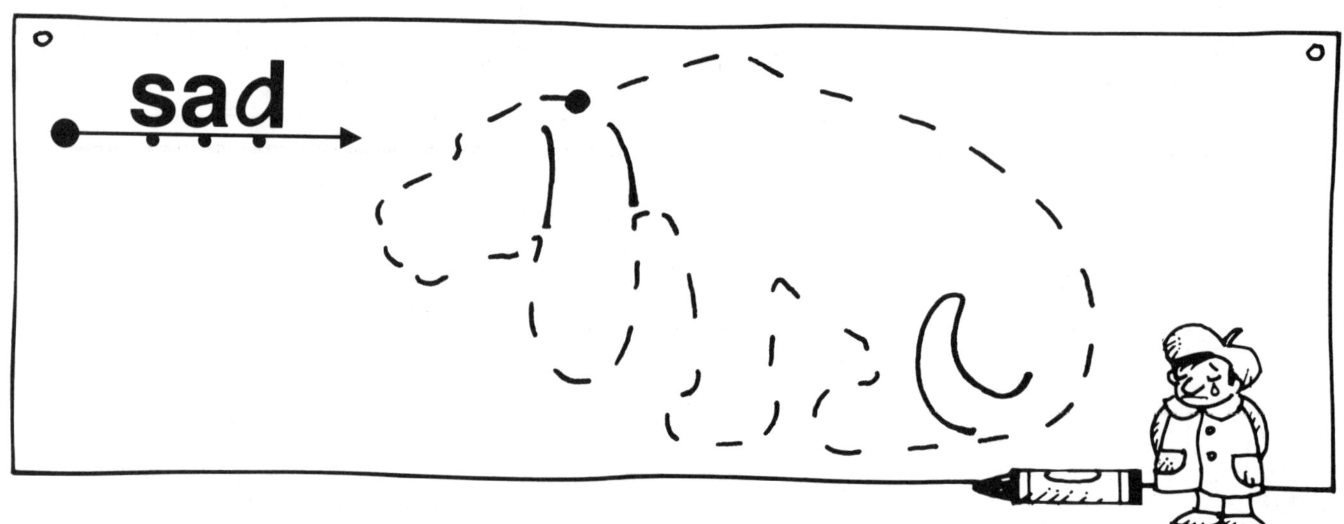

Name ____ **Lesson 45**

Put the pictures in order. In each row, put a *1* by the picture that happens *first*, a *2* by the picture that happens *next*, and a *3* by the picture that happens *last*. When you finish the page, go back and color the pictures.

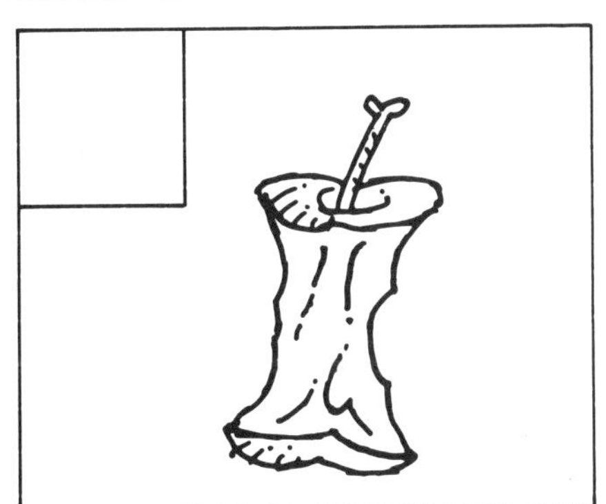

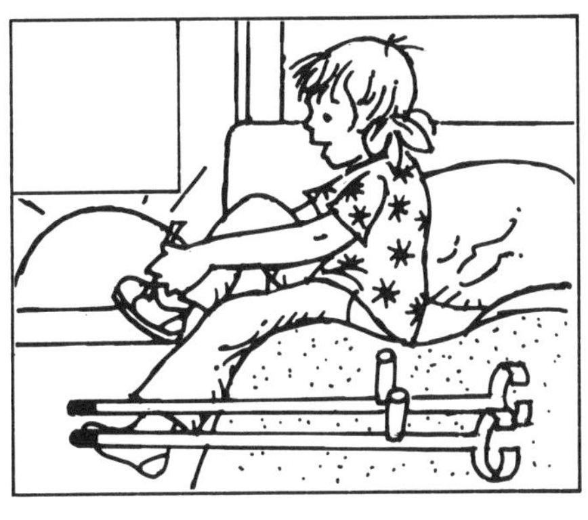

Name ______________________________ **Lesson 46**

Make two picture stories on this page. Cut out the pictures at the bottom of the page. Paste each set of pictures in the right order so they tell a story. The last picture of each story is already in the right place.

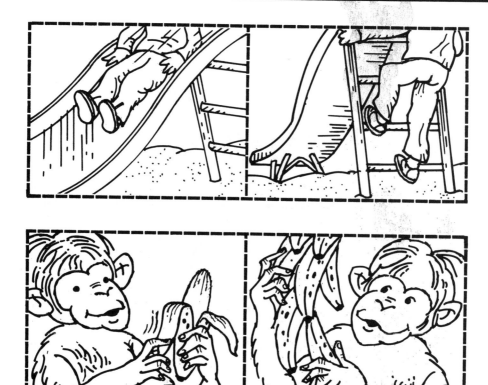

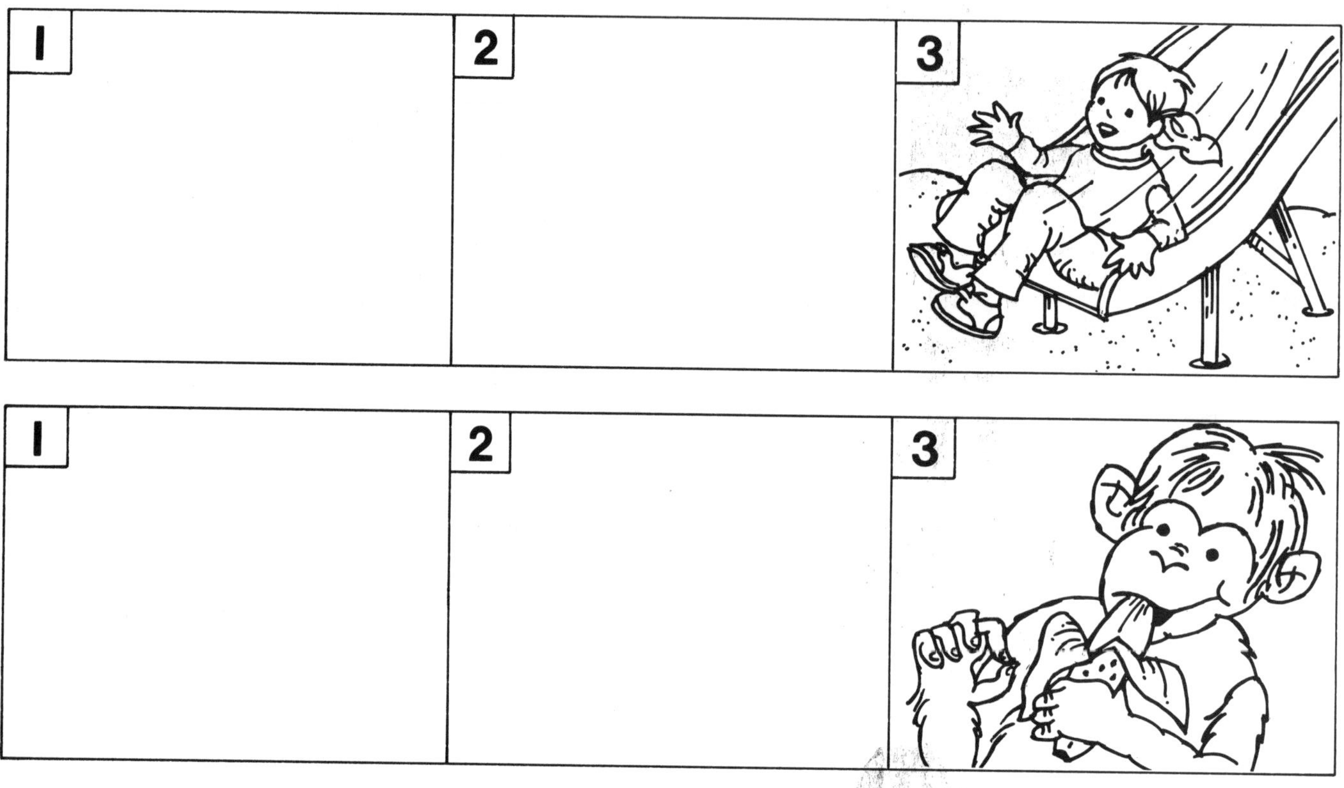

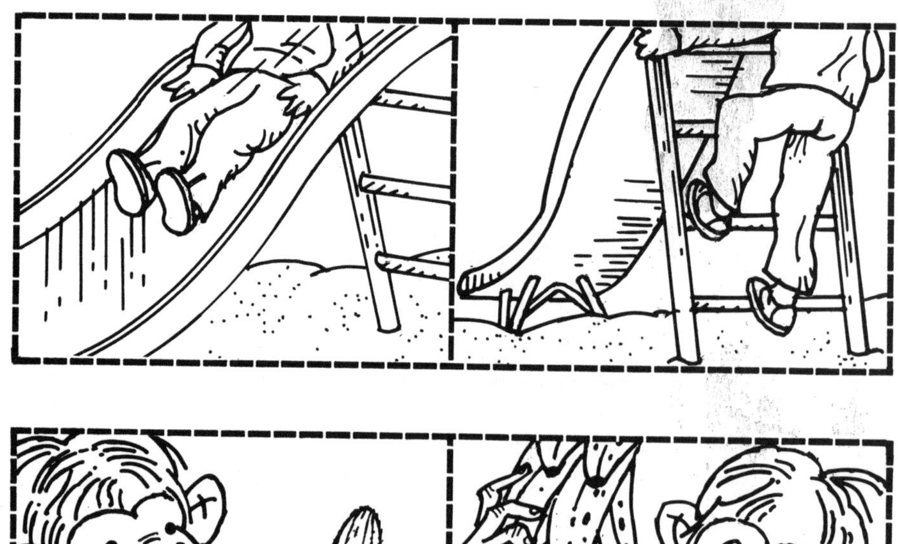

Name ______________________________

Write the words on the page. First trace each word. Then write the word two times by yourself. When you finish, draw a picture of somebody who is *mad*.

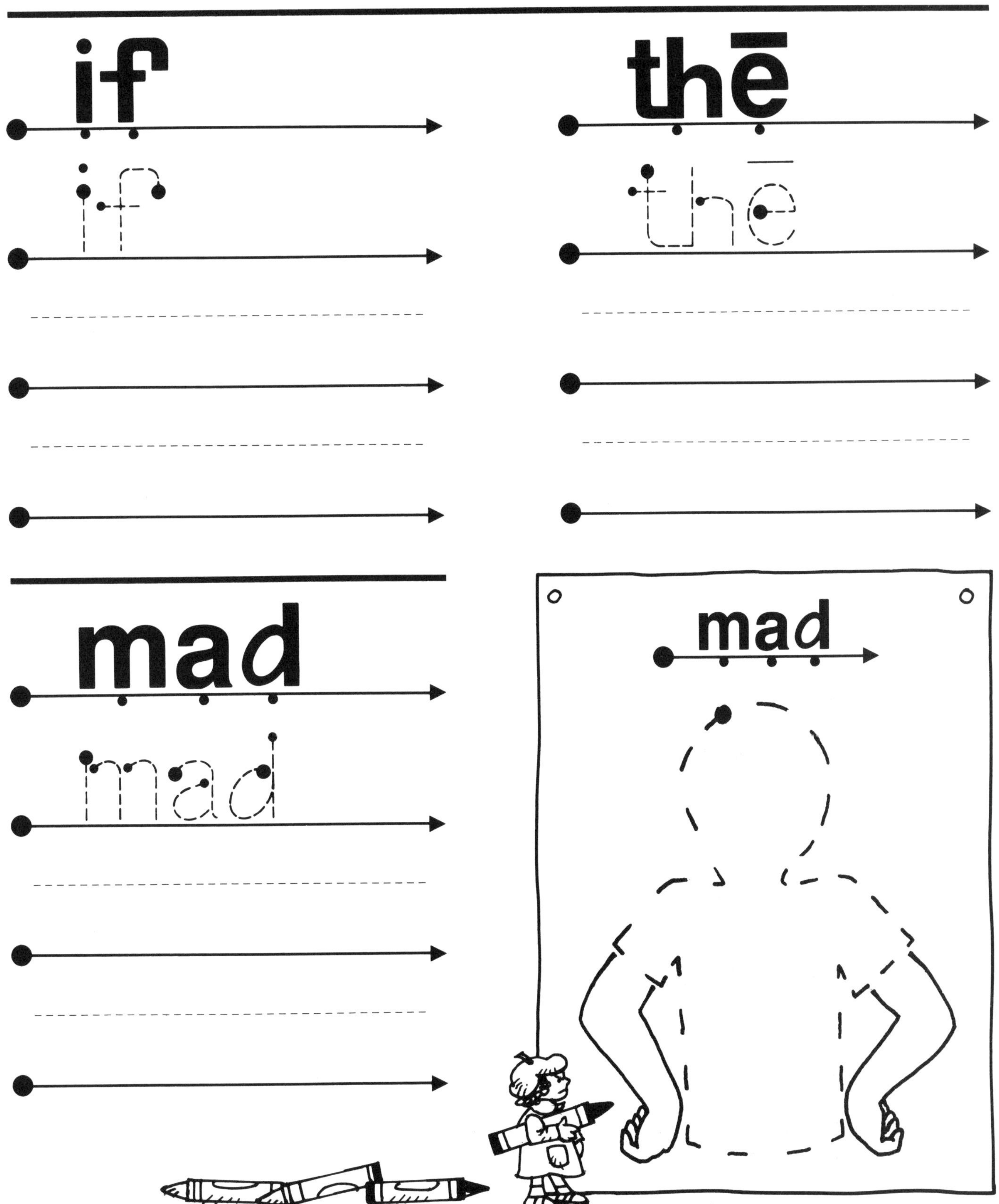

Name ______________________________ Lesson 48

There's an animal hidden on this page. To find the animal, cut out the boxes at the bottom of the page. Cut along the dotted lines. Paste each box on the one that has the same word in it. Color the animal that you find.

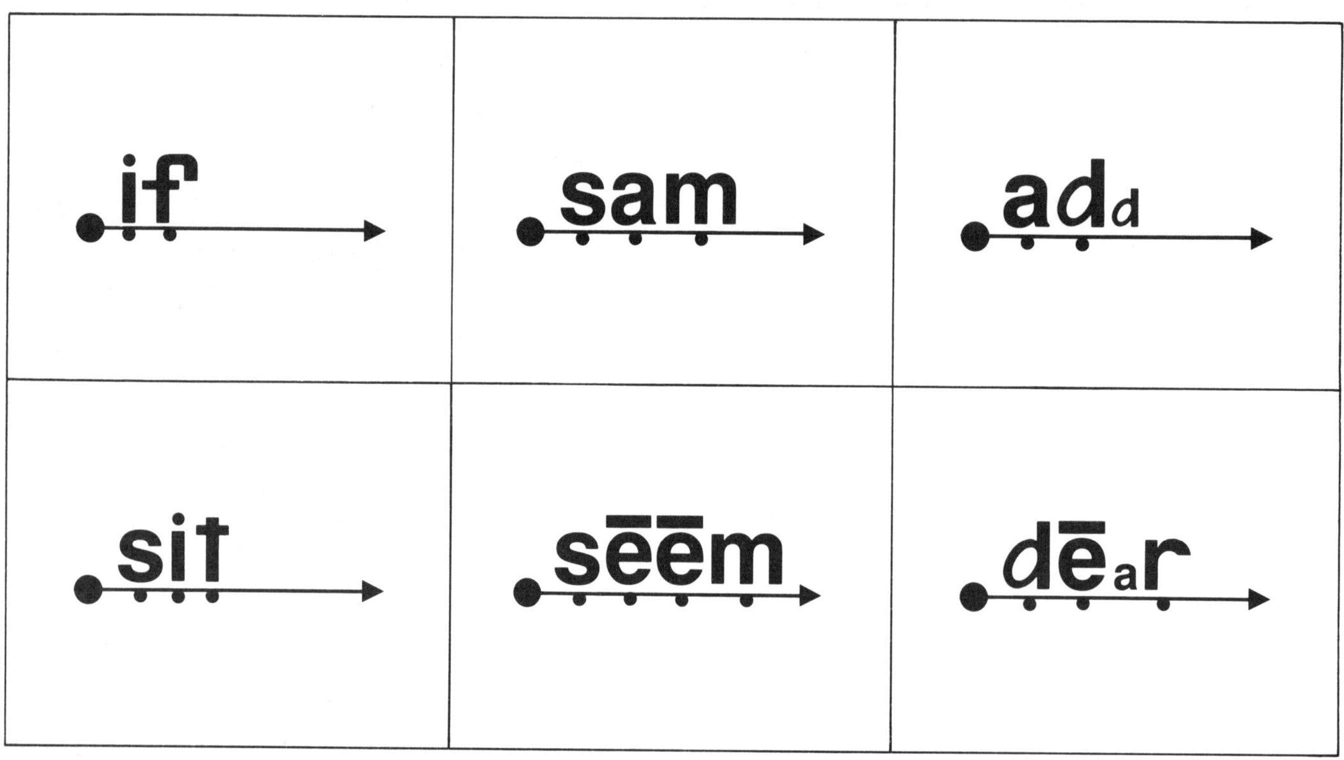

Name ______________________

Make two picture stories on this page. Cut out the pictures at the bottom of the page. Paste each set of pictures in the right order so they tell a story. The last picture of each story is already in the right place.

Help the sentence worms make sentences. Cut out the words at the bottom of the page. Paste them on the worm parts so the words make sentences. When you finish, turn your paper over and draw a picture of one of your sentences.

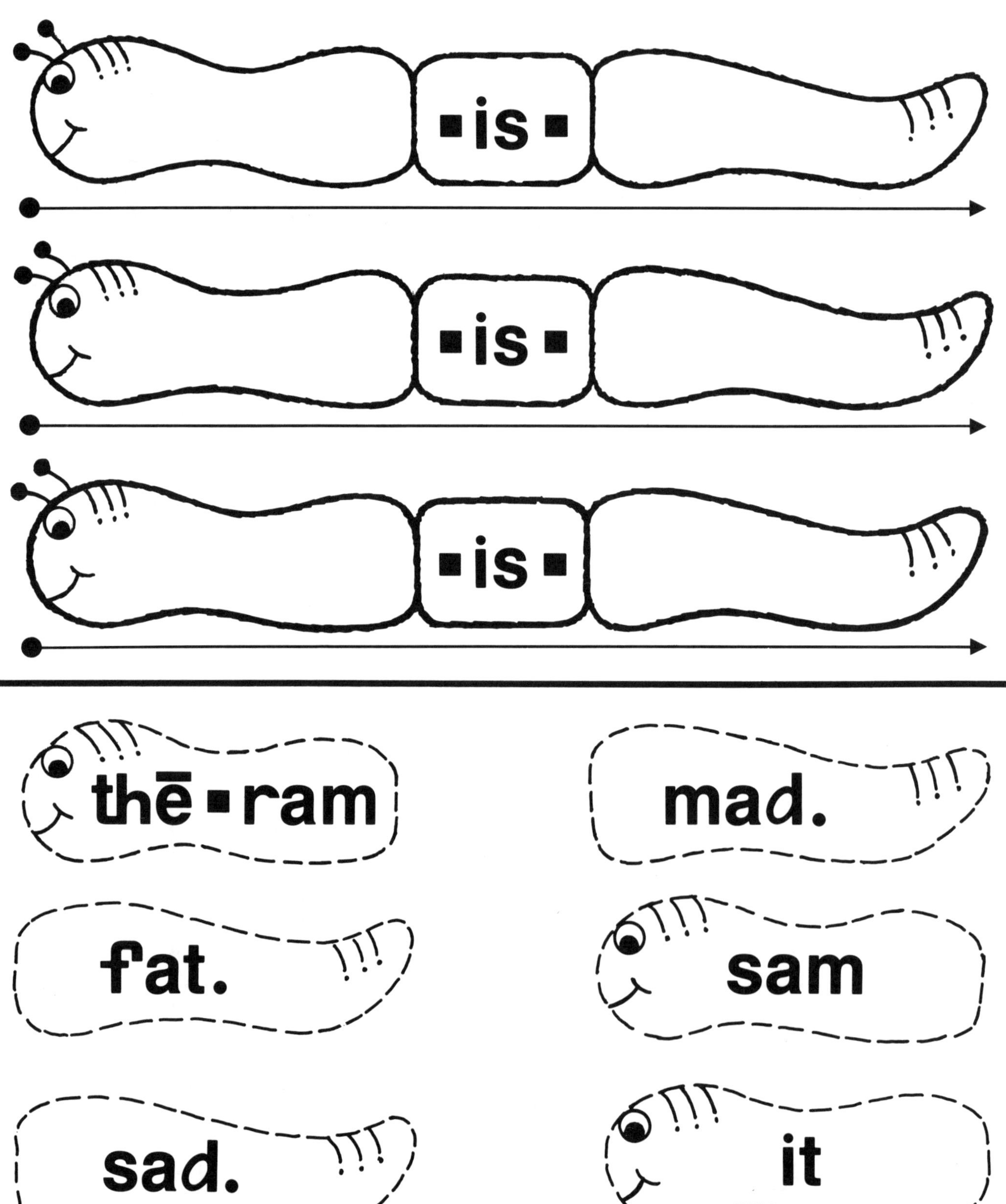

Name ______________________________ Lesson 51

Copy the *t* in each dotted-line box at the bottom of the page. Then cut out the dotted-line boxes. Paste one under each picture whose name begins with *t*.

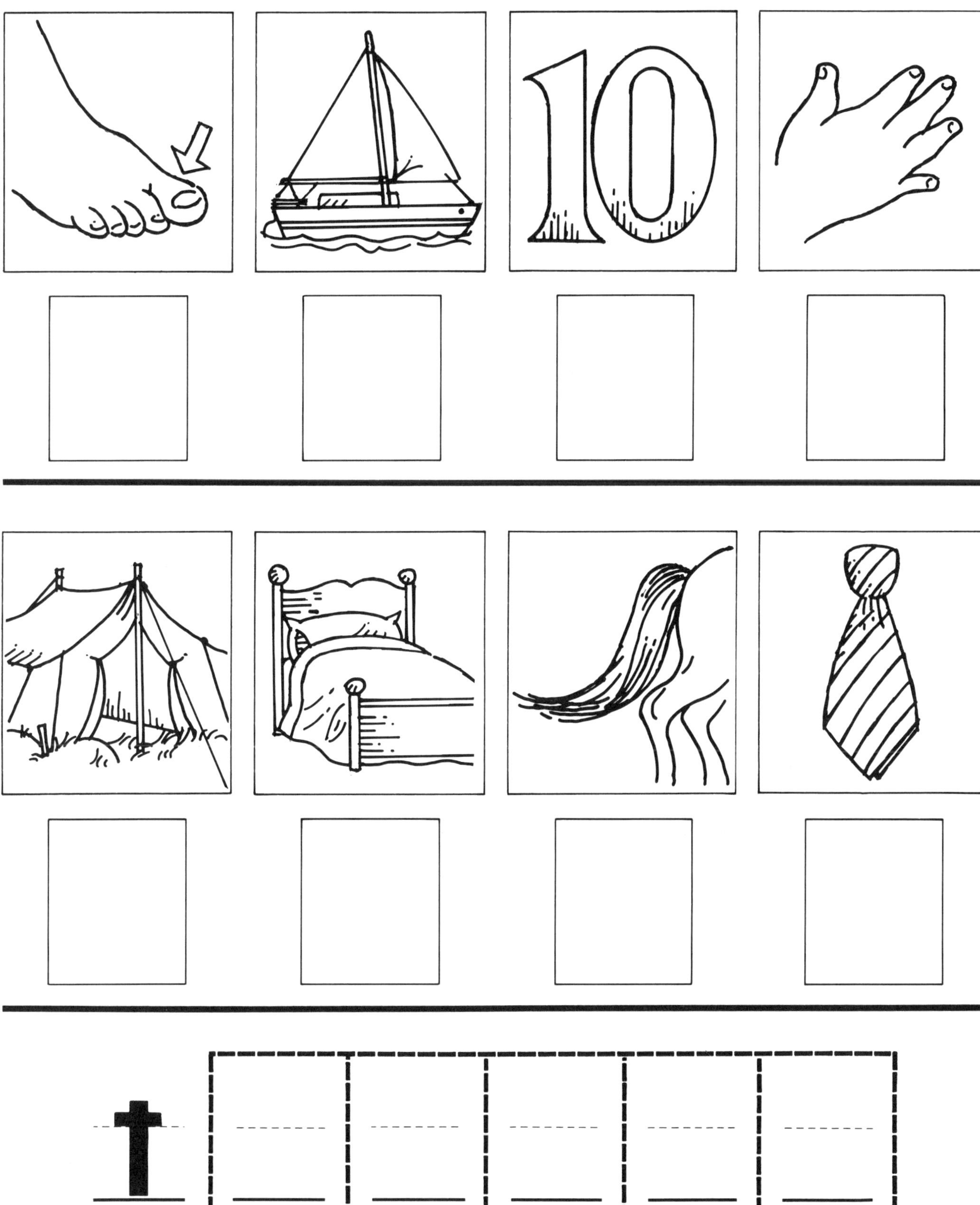

Make two picture stories on this page. Cut out the pictures at the bottom of the page. Paste each set of pictures in the right order so they tell a story. The last picture of each story is already in the right place.

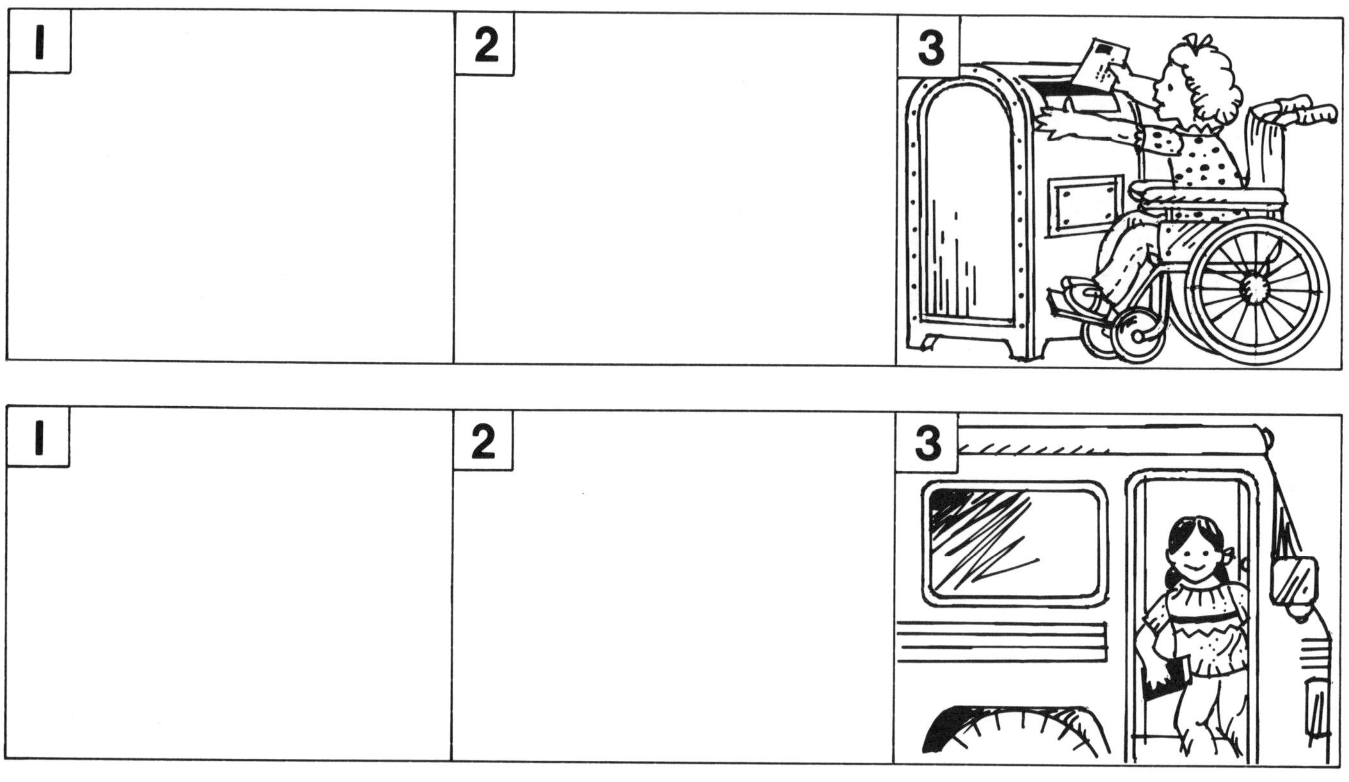

Choose the right words to go with each picture. Write those words on the line. When you finish, color the pictures.

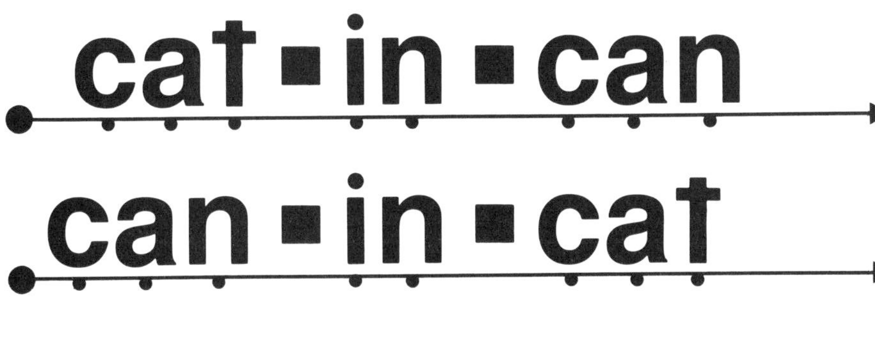

cat ▪ in ▪ can

can ▪ in ▪ cat

_____ ▪ _____ ▪ _____

man ▪ on ▪ ram

ram ▪ on ▪ man

_____ ▪ _____ ▪ _____

sam ▪ in ▪ sēēd

sēēd ▪ in ▪ sam

_____ ▪ _____ ▪ _____

Name ____________________

Copy the *nnn* in each dotted-line box at the bottom of the page. Then cut out the dotted-line boxes. Paste one under each picture whose name begins with *nnn*.

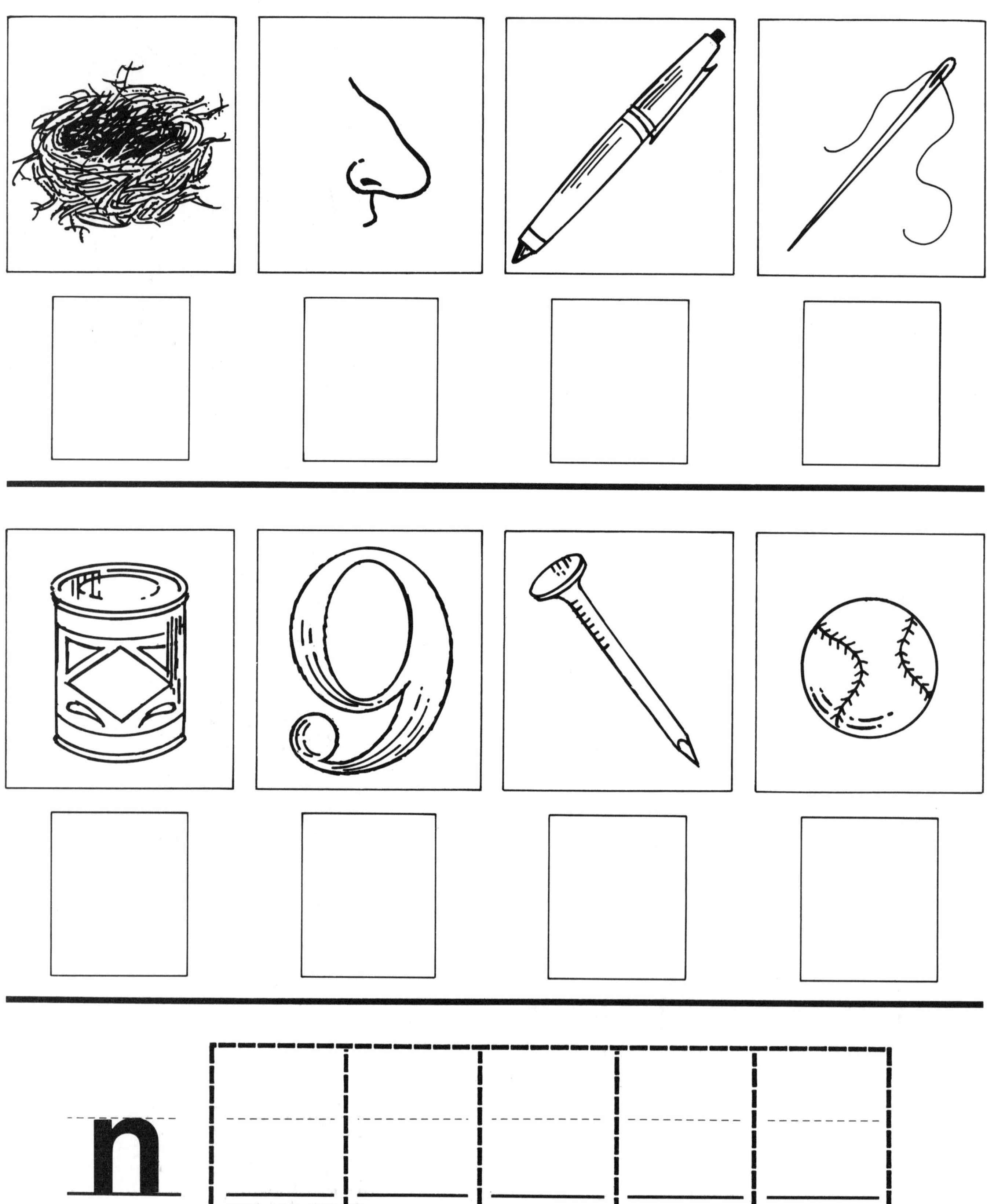

Name ______________________________

Read the word on the arrow at the beginning of each row of letters. That word is hidden in the row of letters. Find the hidden words and circle them. Then draw a picture of the last word—*sam*.

dim	d	i	m	i	d	d	m	d
mad	a	a	m	a	d	d	m	a
miss	s	s	i	s	m	i	s	s
sēēm	m	m	s	ē	ē	m	s	ē
sit	t	i	s	t	i	s	i	t
at	t	a	a	t	t	a	a	a
sēē	ē	s	ē	ē	s	s	s	ē
sam	a	s	m	m	s	a	m	m

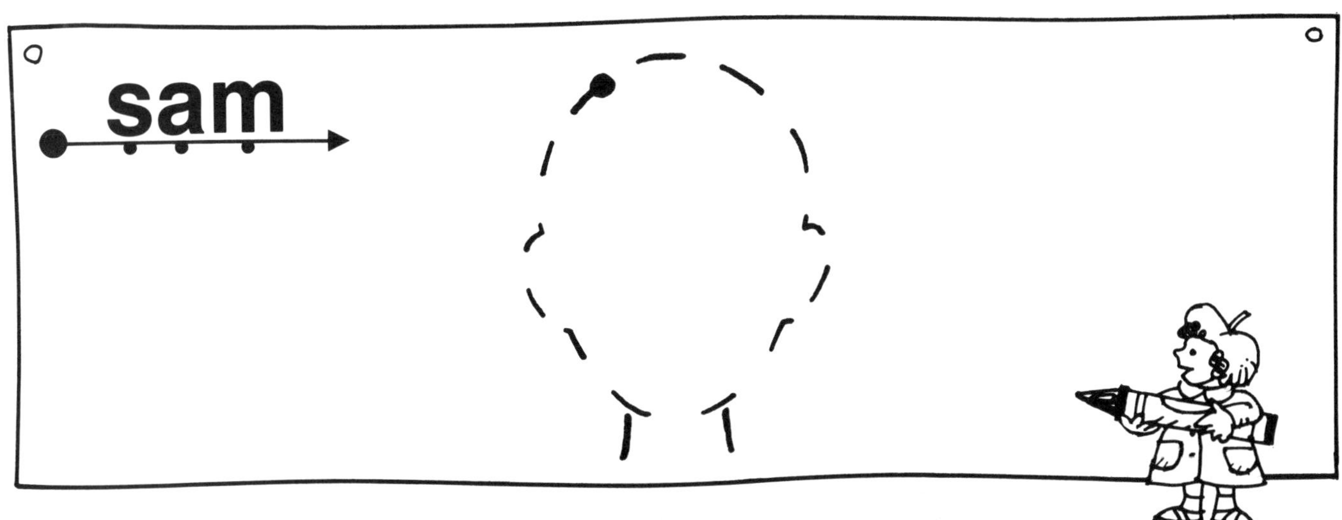

Name ______________________________ Lesson 56

Help the sentence worms make sentences. Cut out the words at the bottom of the page. Paste them on the worm parts so the words make sentences. When you finish, turn your paper over and draw a picture of one of your sentences.

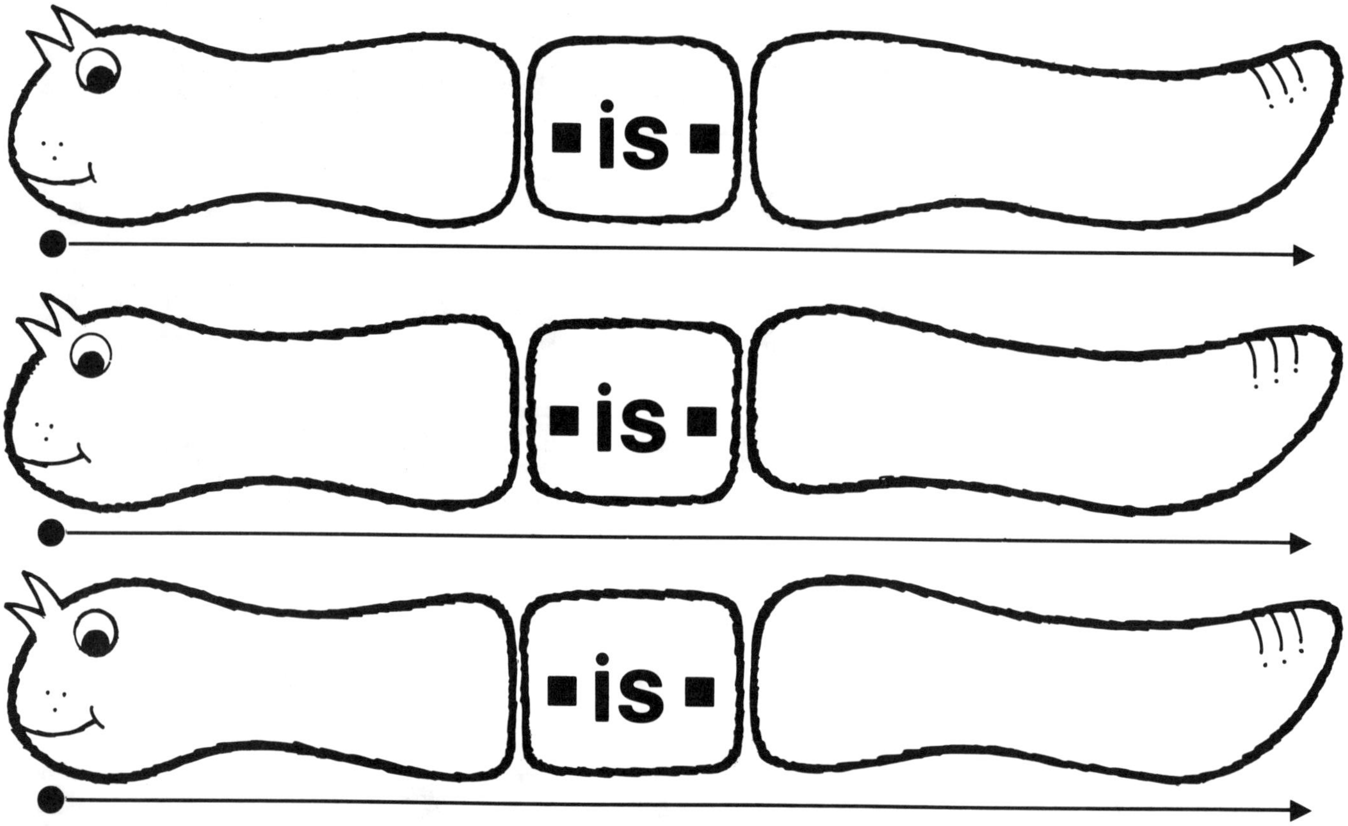

is

is

is

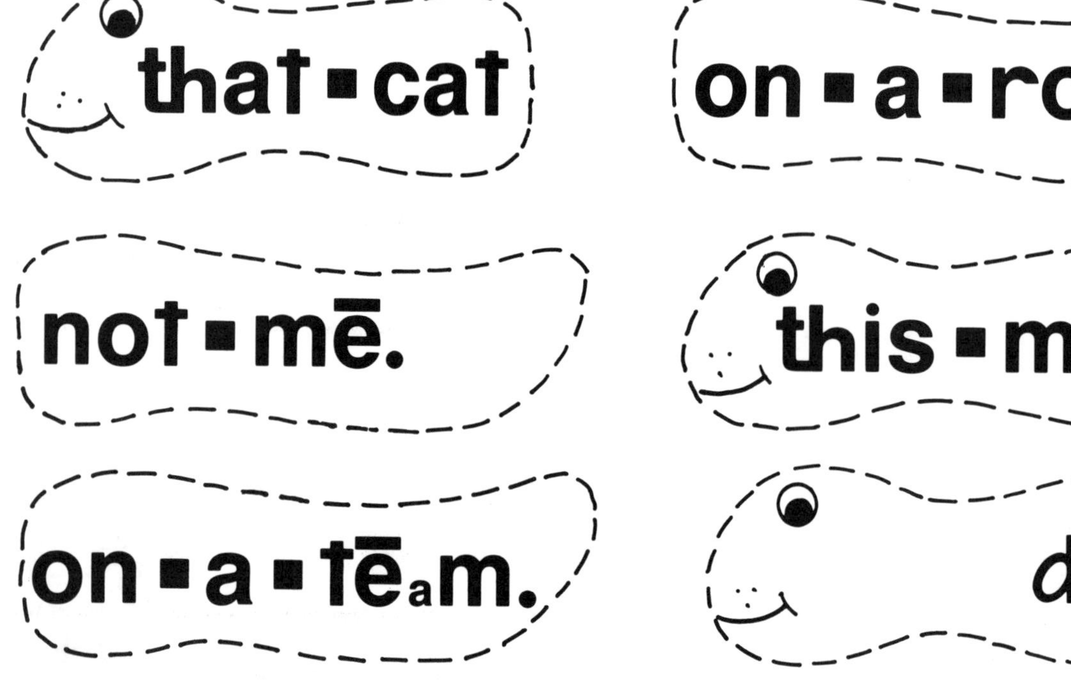

Copy each sentence next to the picture it matches. Then color the pictures.

dan ▪ is ▪ sad.

dan ▪ is ▪ mad.

dan ▪ is ▪ tan.

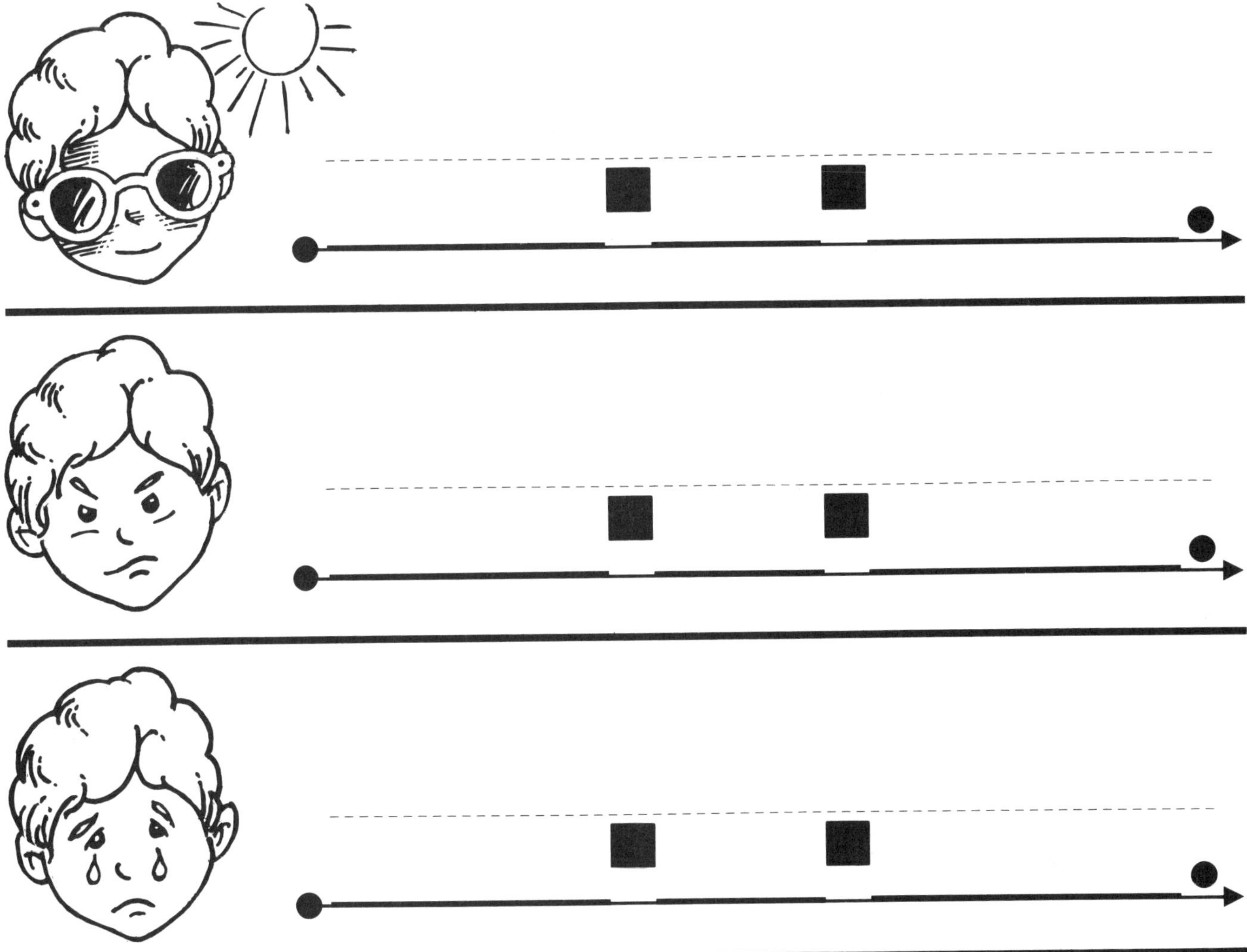

Name ______________________ **Lesson 58**

Copy the *c* in each dotted-line box at the bottom of the page. Then cut out the dotted-line boxes. Paste one under each picture whose name begins with *c*.

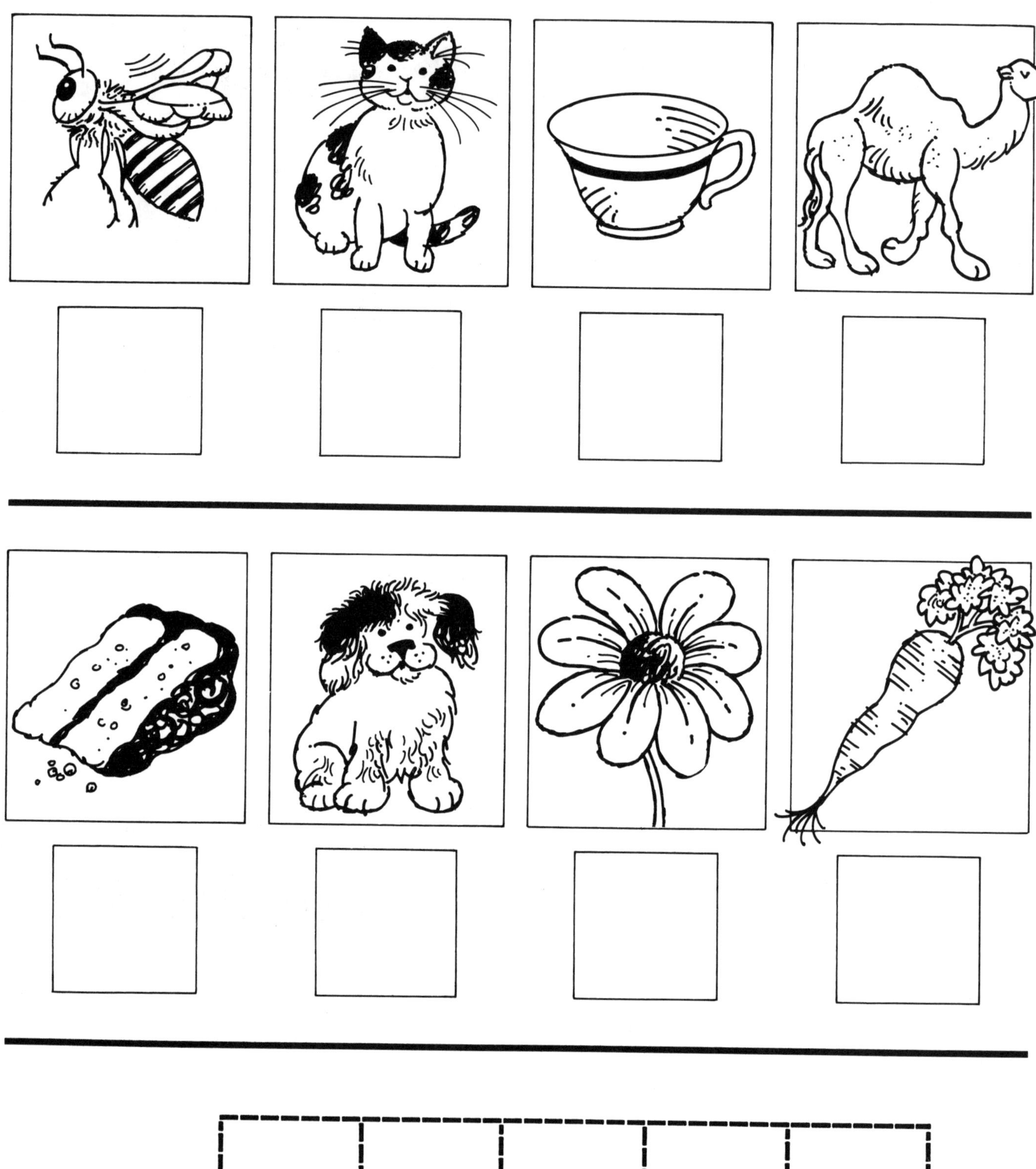

c

Name ________________________________

Write the sentences on the page. First trace each sentence. Then write the sentence by yourself. When you finish, draw a picture of a *sad cat*.

Name ______________________________________

Read the word on the arrow at the beginning of each row of letters. That word is hidden in the row of letters. Find the hidden words and circle them. Then draw a picture of the last word—*dan*.

fin →	f	i	n	n	f	i	f	n
in →	n	i	i	i	n	n	i	i
tin →	n	i	t	n	i	t	i	n
an →	n	n	a	a	a	n	n	n
sit →	t	s	i	t	i	s	s	t
sēēd →	ē	d	s	ē	ē	d	s	d
ran →	a	n	n	r	a	n	n	r
dan →	n	a	d	a	d	d	a	n

Name ______________________________ Lesson 61

Make each word match the picture next to it. Choose the correct letter from the box and write it in the blank.

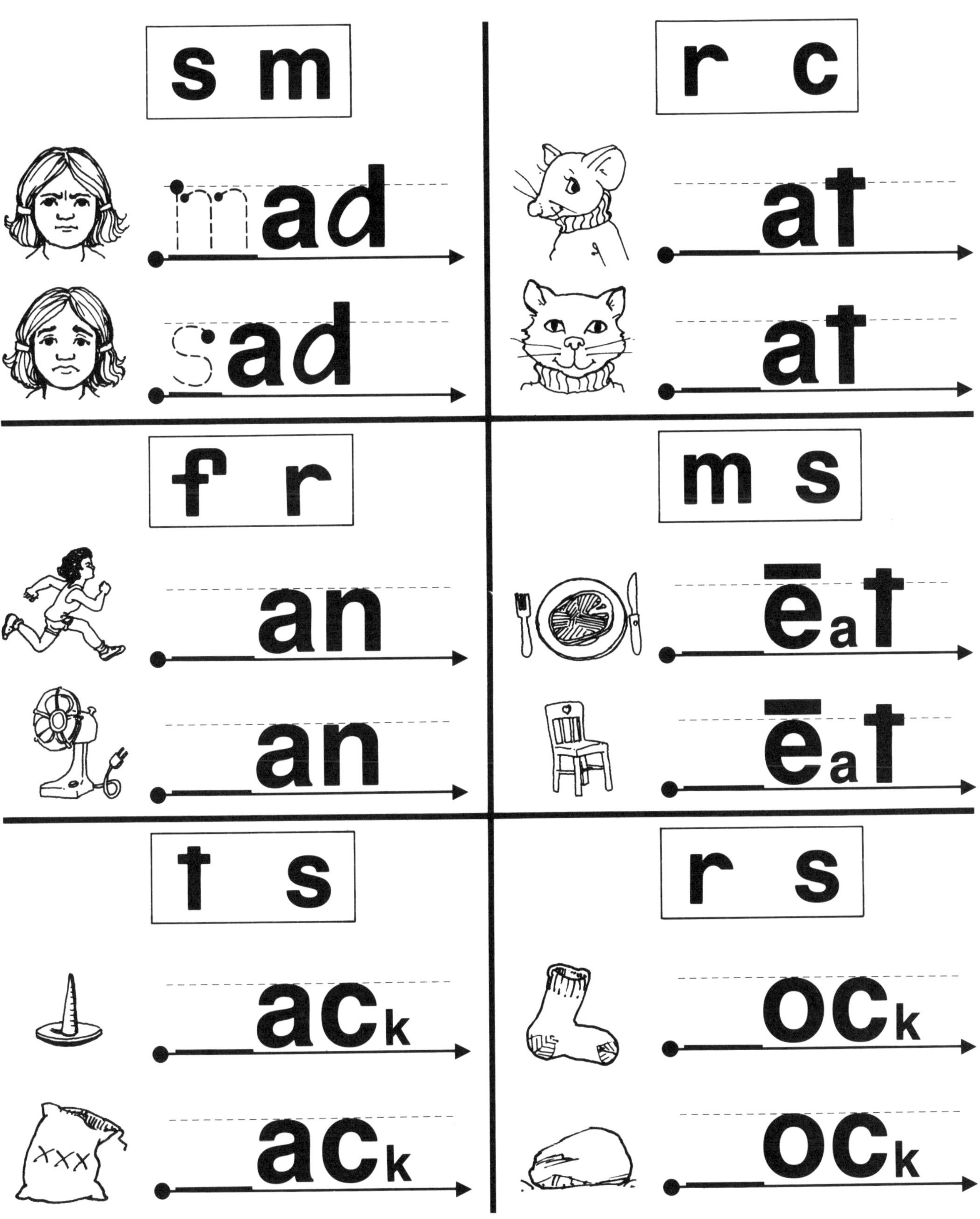

Name ________________________________

Choose the right words to go with each picture. Write those words on the line. When you finish, color the pictures.

dan ▪ on ▪ fēēt

fēēt ▪ on ▪ dan

▪ ▪

rat ▪ on ▪ cat

cat ▪ on ▪ rat

▪ ▪

fin ▪ on ▪ fan

fan ▪ on ▪ fin

▪ ▪

Name ____ **Lesson 63**

Write the sentences on the page. First trace each sentence. Then write the sentence by yourself. When you finish, draw a picture of *a neat sock*.

thē ▪ sock ▪ fit.

▪ ▪ .

it ▪ is ▪ nēat.

it ▪ is ▪ nēat.

▪ ▪ .

neat ▪ sock

Name ____________________

Help the sentence worms make sentences. Cut out the words at the bottom of the page. Paste them on the worm parts so the words make sentences. When you finish, turn your paper over and draw a picture of one of your sentences.

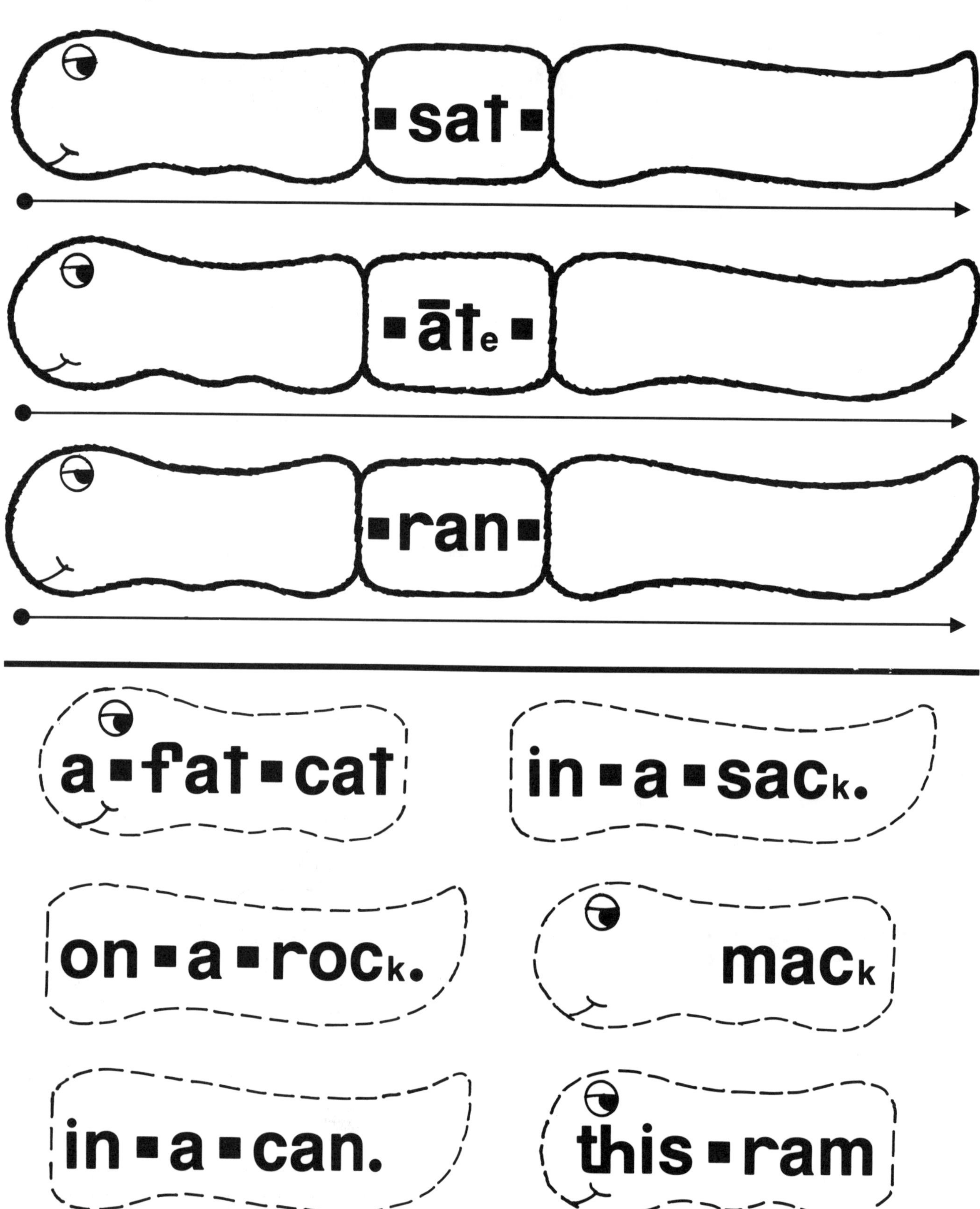

These groups of words don't make sense because they're not in the right order. Put the words in order. Write them in the boxes. Then finish the pictures so they show what the words say.

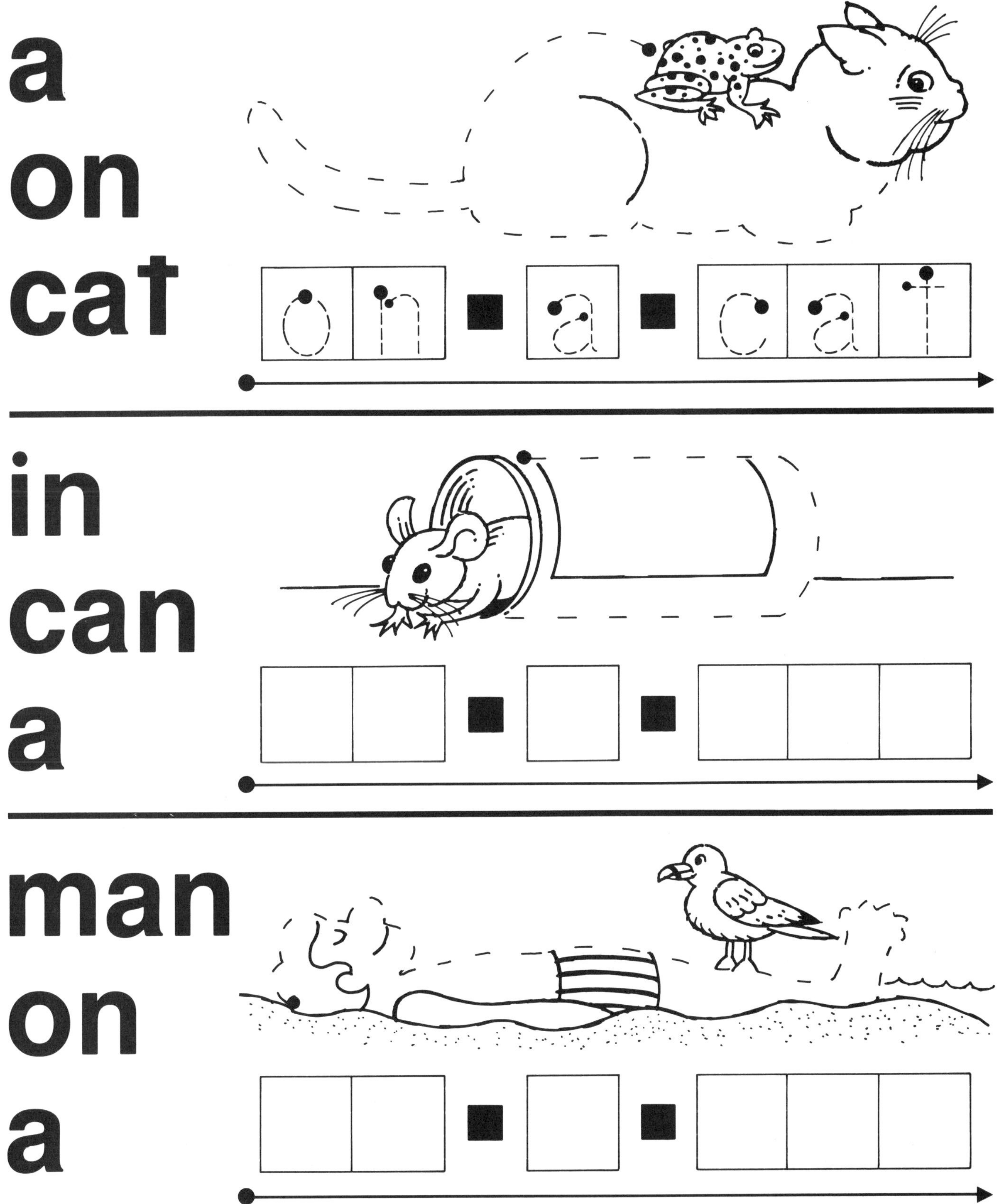

Name ____________________

Cut out the words at the bottom of the page. Paste each word in the box next to the picture it matches. Then copy the words.

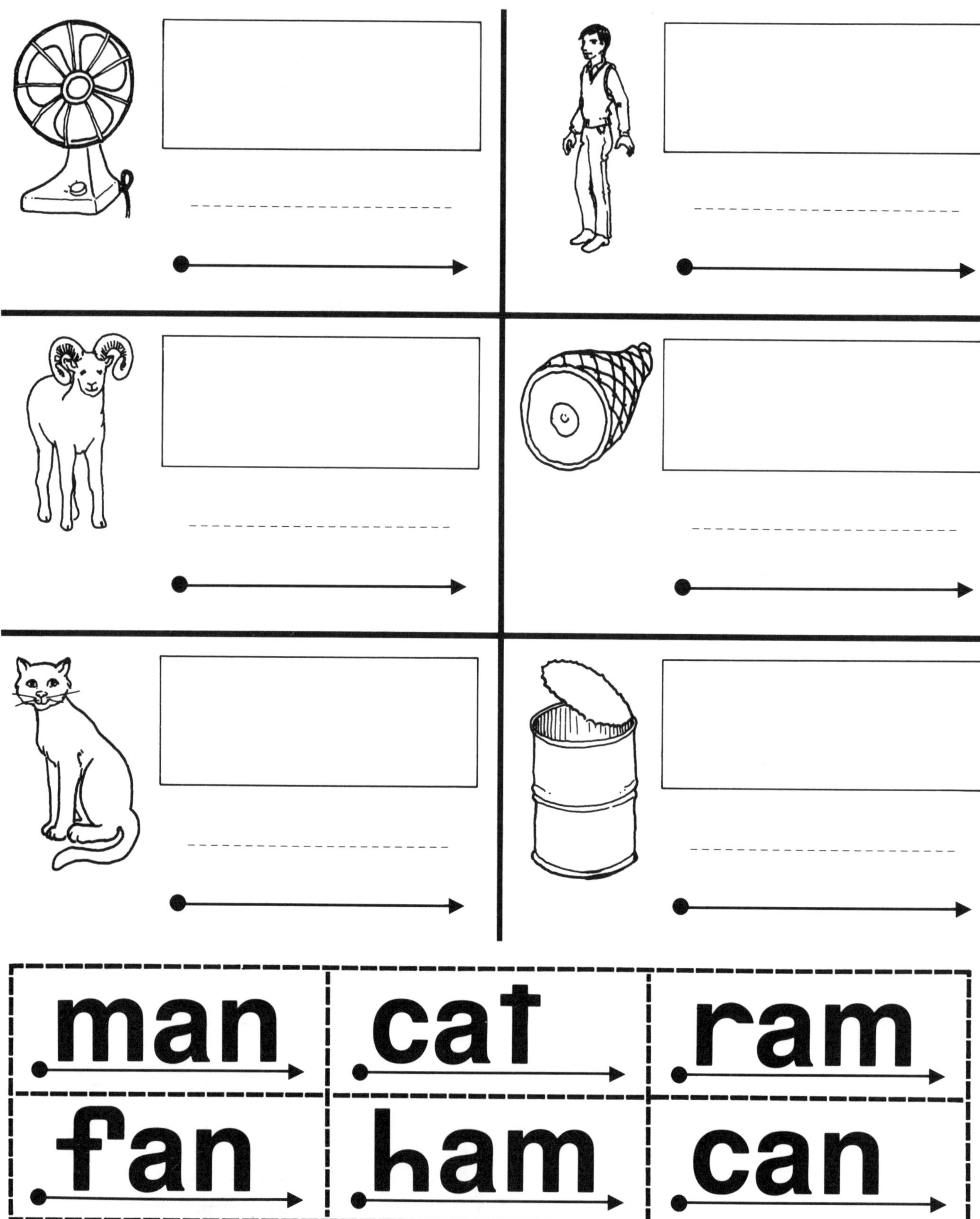

man	cat	ram
fan	ham	can

Name ________________________________ Lesson 67

Copy each sentence next to the picture it matches. Then color the pictures.

thē ▪ cat ▪ sat.

thē ▪ cat ▪ ran.

thē ▪ cat ▪ fit.

Name ________________________________

Make each word match the picture next to it. Choose the correct letter from the box and write it in the blank.

h r

___am

___am

s r

___un

___un

s h

___it

___it

c m

___an

___an

s f

___ēēd

___ēēd

t f

___ēar

___ēar

Name ______________________________ Lesson 69

These groups of words don't make sense because they're not in the right order. Put the words in order. Write them in the boxes. Then finish the pictures so they show what the words say.

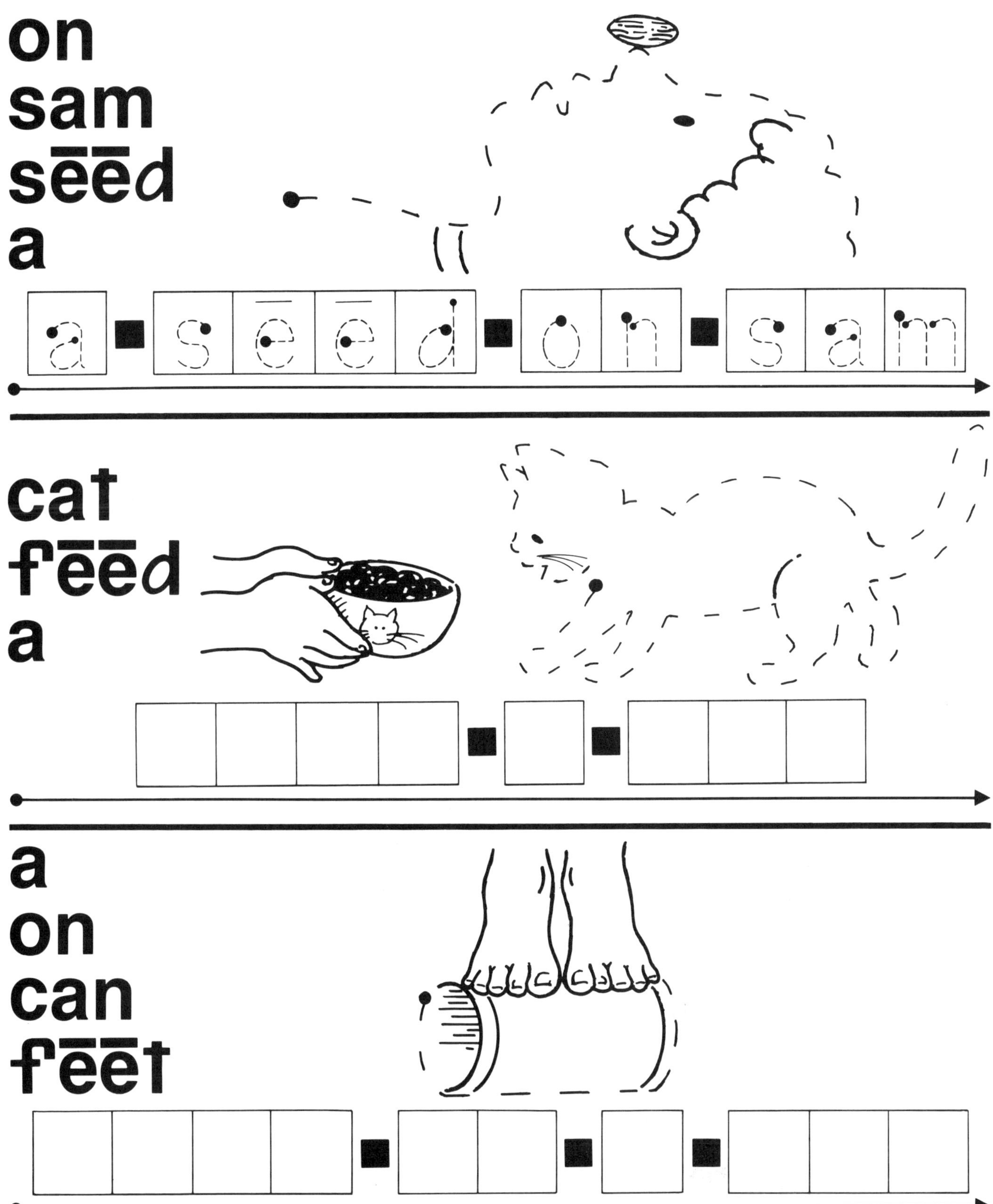

Name ______________________________ Lesson 70

Look at each picture and read the sentences below it. Circle the sentence that tells about the picture. When you finish, color all the pictures.

sam ▪ is ▪ mad.

sam ▪ is ▪ sick.

dan ▪ had ▪ a ▪ sack.

dan ▪ had ▪ a ▪ tack.

hē ▪ can ▪ rock.

hē ▪ can ▪ hit.

it ▪ is ▪ on ▪ a ▪ seat.

it ▪ is ▪ on ▪ a ▪ sock.

Name ____________________ **Lesson 71**

Write *h* under each picture whose name begins with *h*. When you finish, color the pictures you wrote *h* under.

h

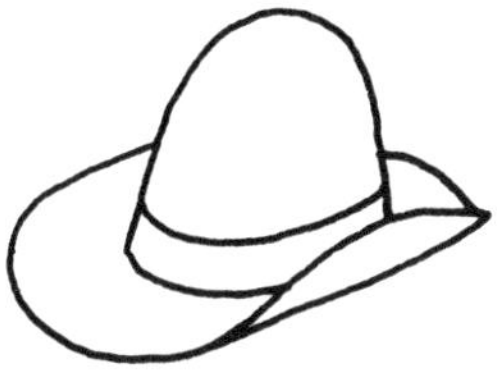

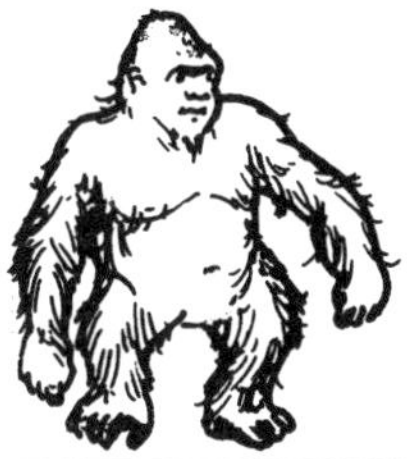

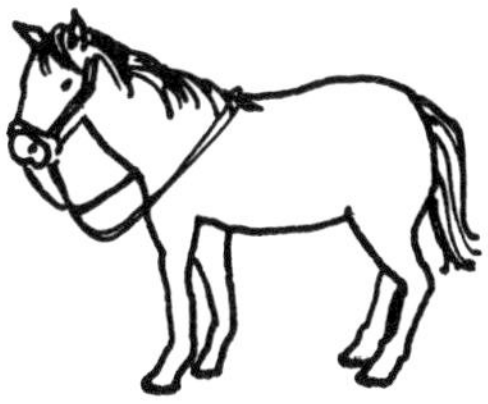

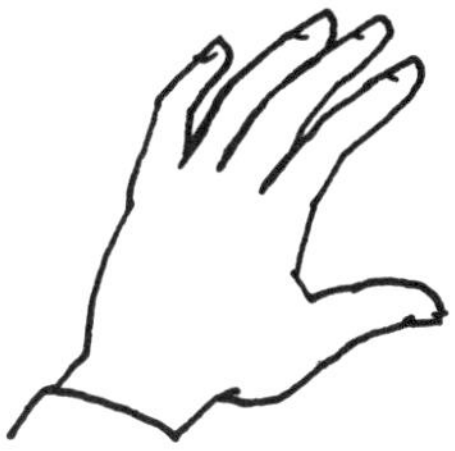

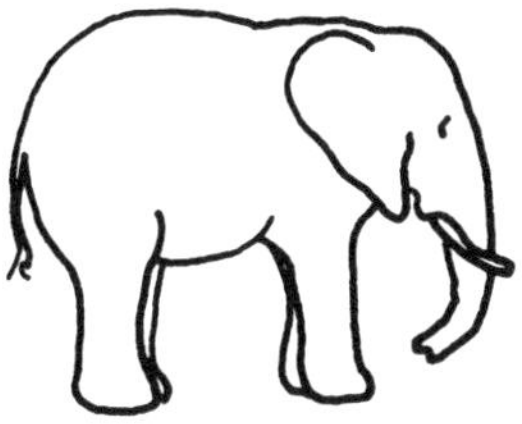

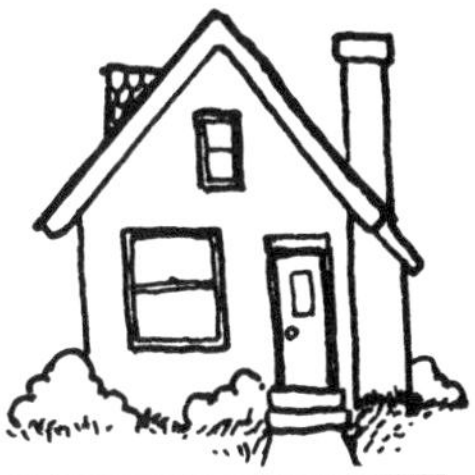

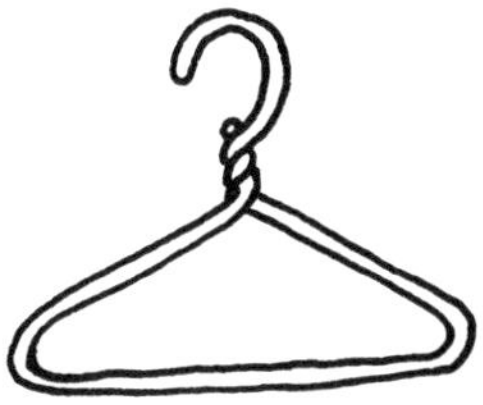

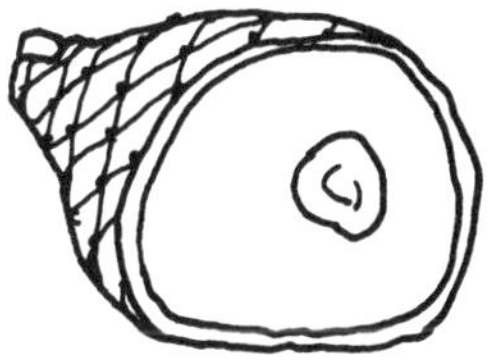

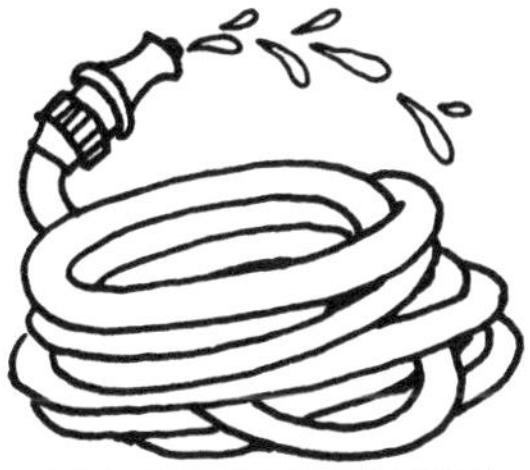

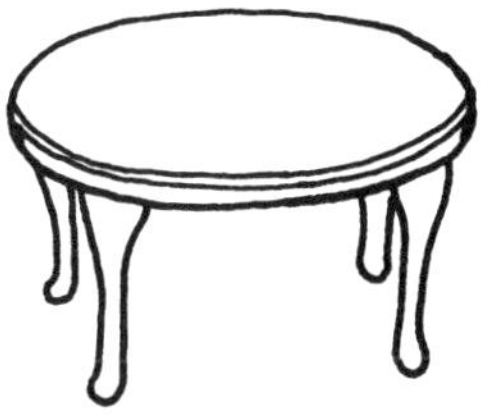

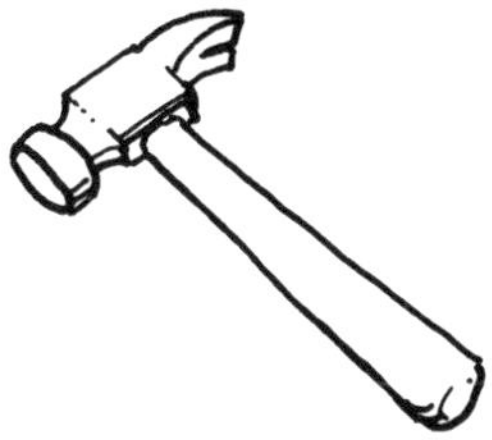

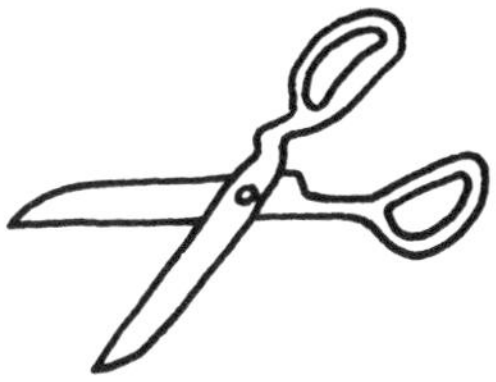

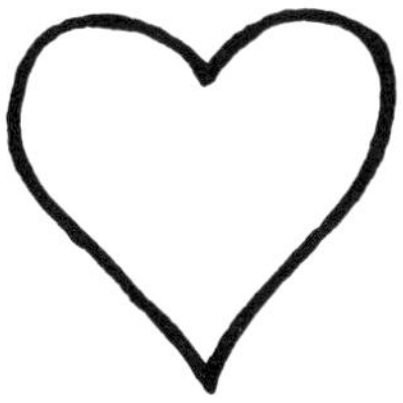

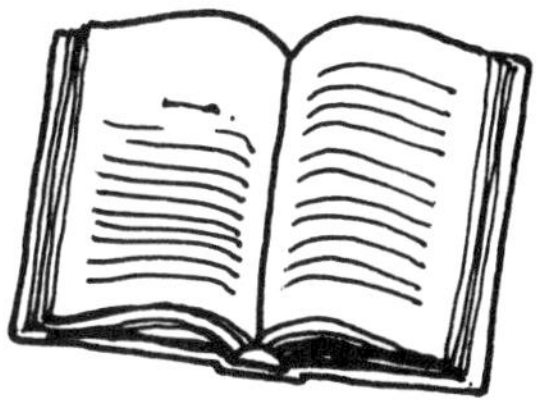

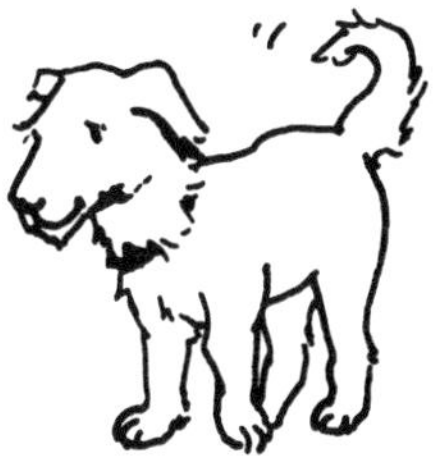

Cut out the words at the bottom of the page. Paste each word at the end of the sentence it finishes.

dan ▪ āte ▪ a ▪ [ ].

mack ▪ is ▪ his ▪ [ ].

a ▪ cat ▪ sat ▪ in ▪ thē ▪ [ ].

sam ▪ is ▪ on ▪ a ▪ [ ].

thē ▪ mēat ▪ is ▪ [ ].

nāme	nut	hot	tēam	sun

Name ______________________________ **Lesson 73**

These groups of words don't make sense because they're not in the right order. Put the words in order. Write them in the boxes. Then finish the pictures so they show what the words say.

fēēt
mud
in

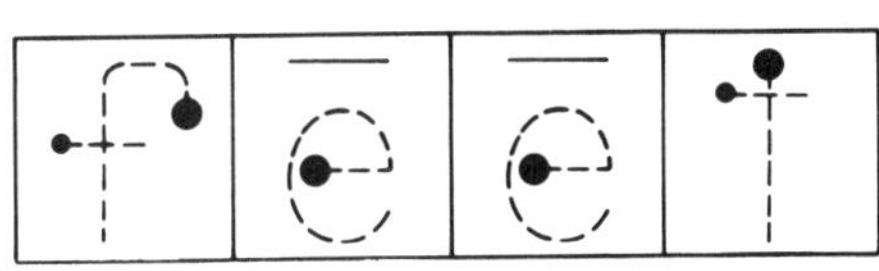

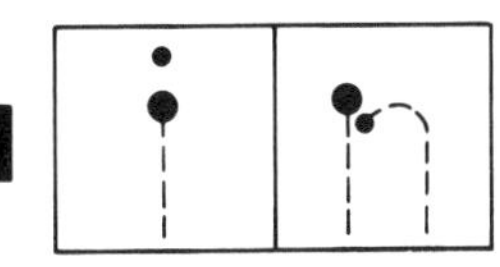

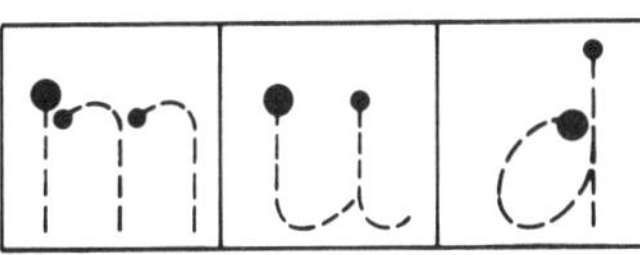

sēēd
on
rug
a

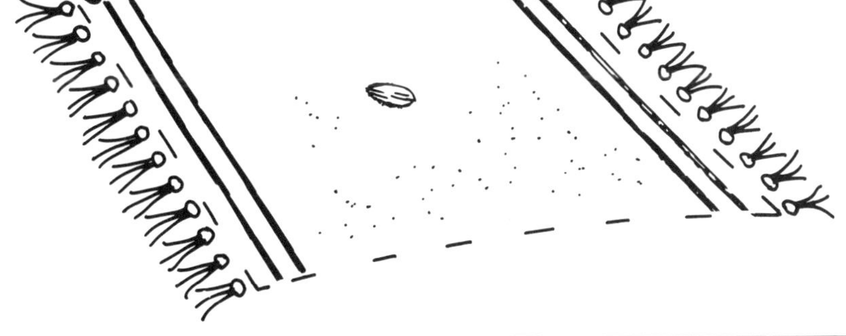

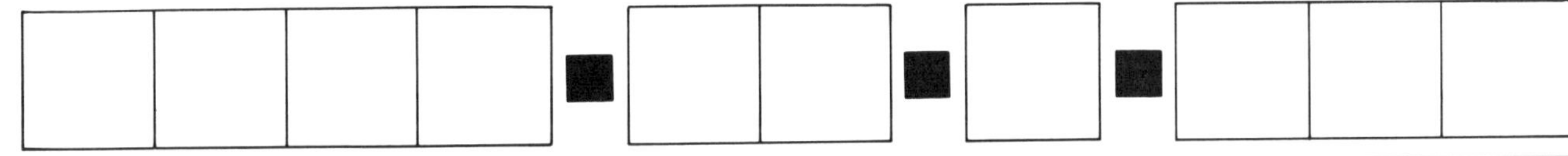

mitt
a
has
hē

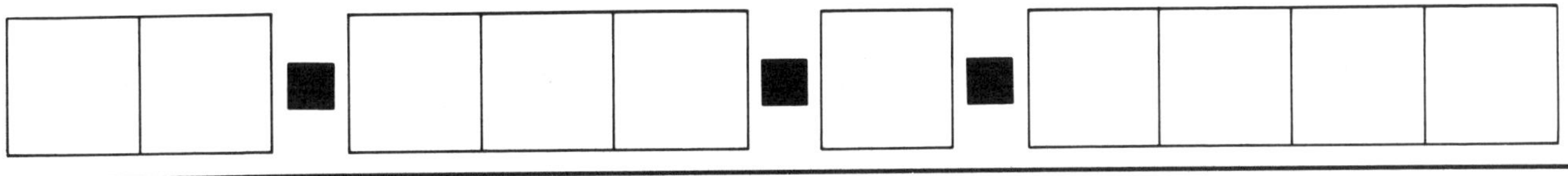

Name ______________________________

Copy the word that goes with each picture. Then color all the pictures.

hut
hot

cat
rat

rug
ram

fun
sun

not
nut

fēēt
fēēd

Name ____

Look at each picture and read the sentences below it. Circle the sentence that tells about the picture.
When you finish, color all the pictures.

it is hot.

it is not hot.

hē is on a rock.

hē is on a fan.

mack is mēan.

mack is sad.

dan has a fin.

dan has a fan.

Name ______________________________ Lesson 76

Copy each sentence next to the picture it matches. Then color the pictures.

sam ▪ is ▪ a ▪ cat.

sam ▪ is ▪ a ▪ man.

sam ▪ is ▪ a ▪ ram.

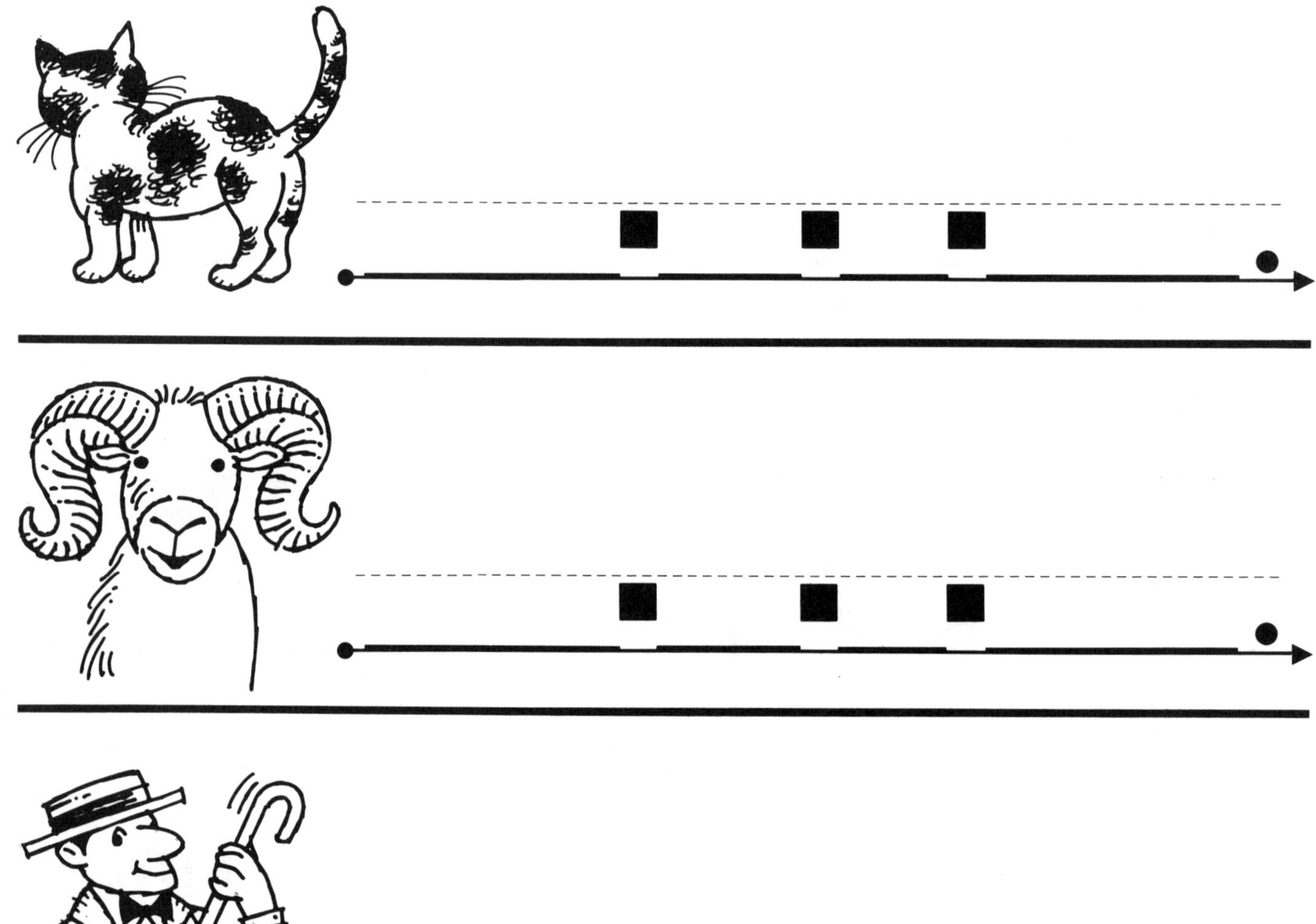

Name ______________________________

Trace the words on the page. The words tell you things you *might* find in the picture. Look for those things in the picture. Copy the words for the things you find.

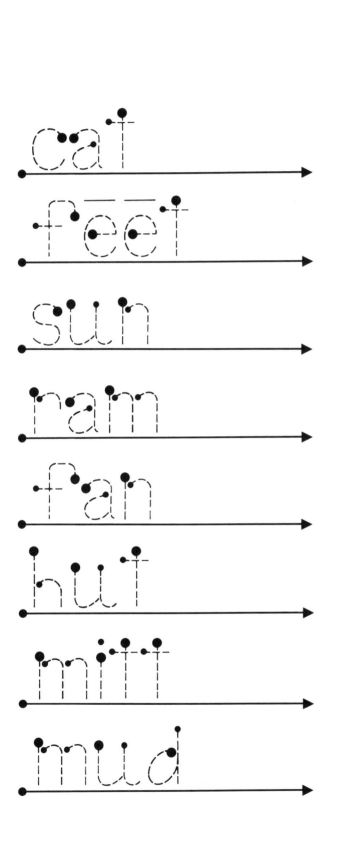

cat

feet

sun

ram

fan

hut

mitt

mud

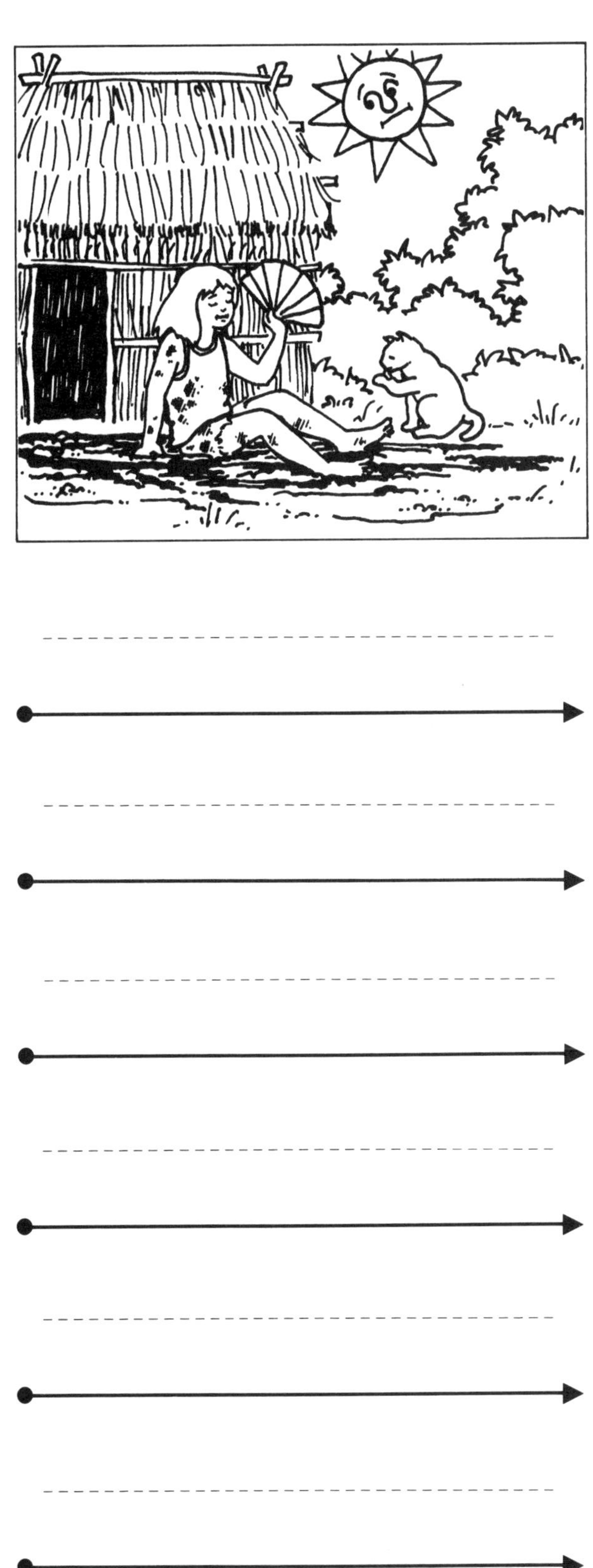

Name ______________________________ Lesson 78

Copy the word that goes with each picture. Then color all the pictures.

ant

am

dim

dan

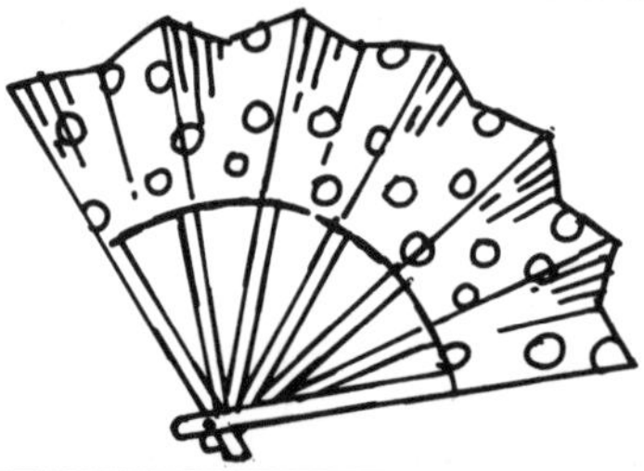

fat

fan

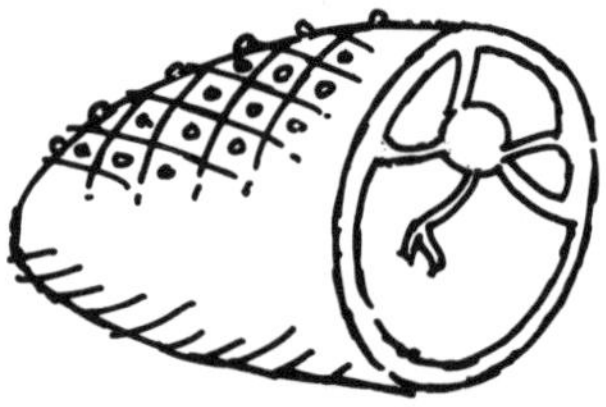

ham

has

miss

mitt

ran

ram

Cut out the words at the bottom of the page. Paste each word at the end of the sentence it finishes.

sam ▪ ran ▪ in ▪ thē ▪  .

hē ▪ āte ▪ hot ▪ ______ .

thē ▪ ram ▪ has ▪ fat ▪ ______ .

thē ▪ sock ▪ will ▪ not ▪ ______ .

mack ▪ sat ▪ on ▪ a ▪ ______ .

mud	fit	fēēt	rock	mēat

Name ______________________________ **Lesson 80**

Make the sentences match the pictures. Circle the right word to finish each sentence. When you finish, color the pictures.

sam ▪ is ▪

sad. mad. fat.

mack ▪ has ▪ a ▪

cat. hat. fat.

dan ▪ is ▪ a ▪ mēan ▪

man. fan. tan.

a ▪ ram ▪ is ▪ in ▪

sun. mud. hut.

a ▪ cat ▪ āte ▪ a ▪

sam. ham. ram.

Name ____

Help the sentence trains make sentences. Cut out the words at the bottom of the page. Paste them on the train parts so the words make sentences. When you finish, turn your paper over and draw a picture of one of your sentences.

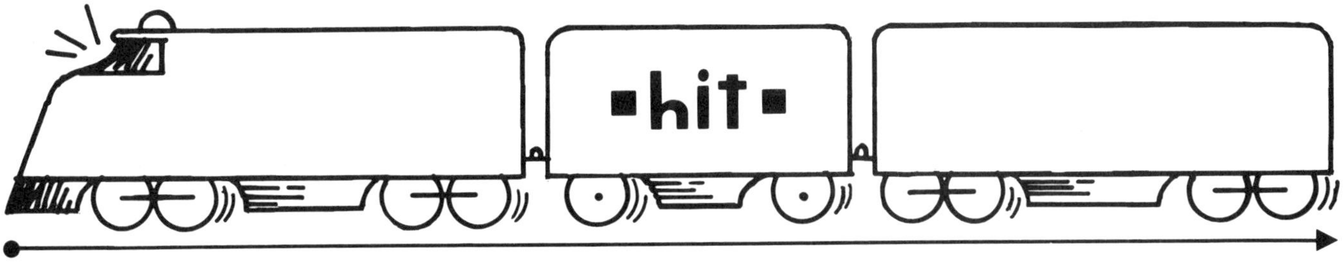

hit

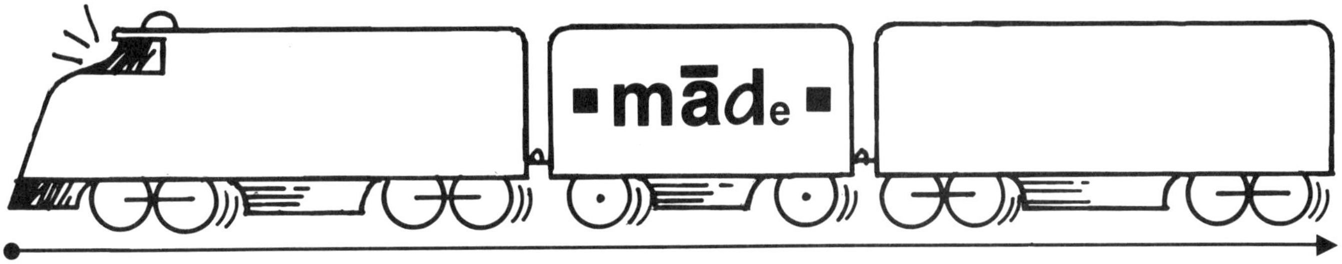

māde

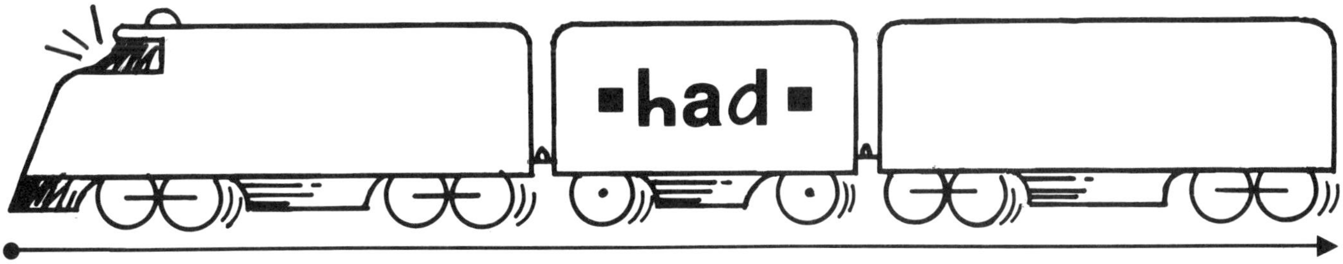

had

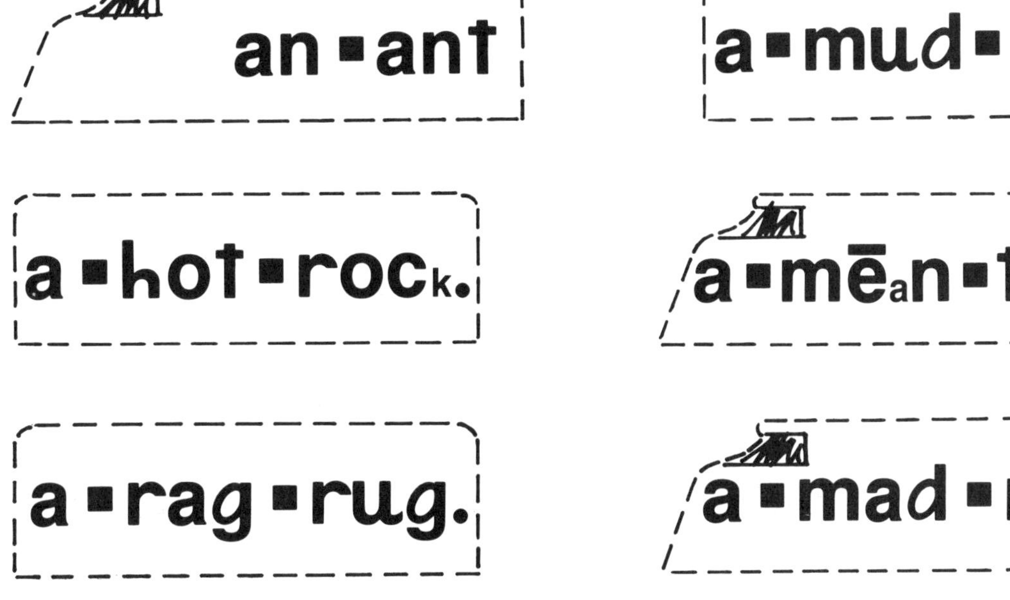

Name ______________________________ Lesson 82

Read the word on the arrow at the beginning of each row of letters. That word is hidden in the row of letters. Find the hidden words and circle them. Then draw a picture of the last two words—*his hand.*

rut →	r	r	u	t	l	g	u	t	r
fig →	ā	o	f	n	g	f	i	g	i
nut →	i	f	n	u	t	t	u	n	m
sag →	s	a	g	s	m	a	g	t	g
run →	ē	n	r	i	r	u	n	l	r
ant →	t	n	a	n	m	a	a	n	t
his →	f	h	h	i	s	u	s	d	i
hand →	d	h	u	h	a	n	d	o	h

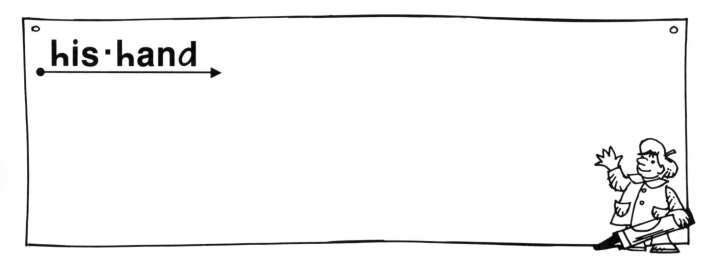

his·hand →

Name ____________________

These groups of words don't make sense because they're not in the right order. Put the words in order. Write them in the boxes. Then finish the pictures so they show what the words say.

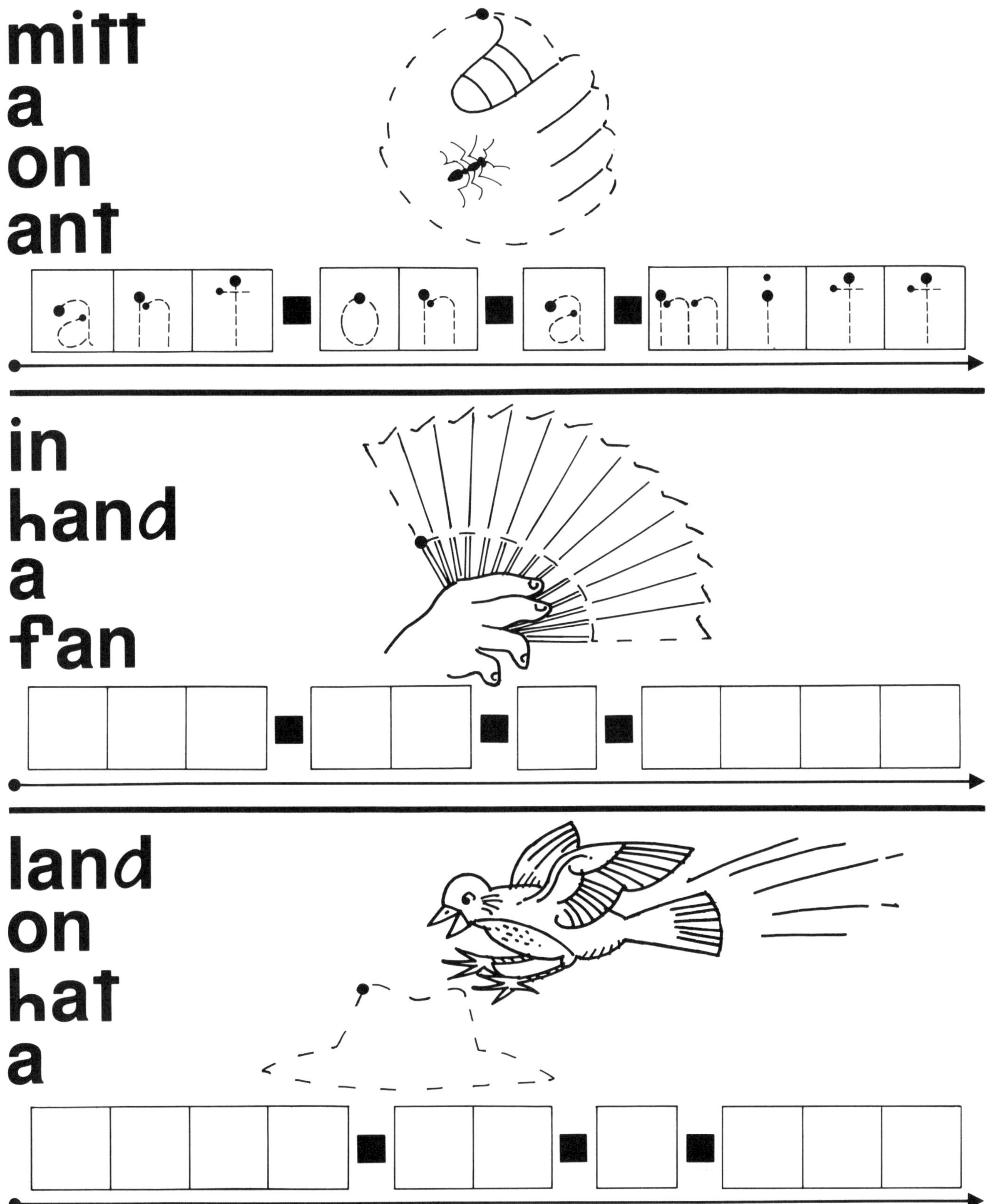

Name ______________________________ Lesson 84

There's a part missing from each picture on this page. Read the sentences to find out what parts are missing. Draw in the missing parts. Then color all the pictures.

wē·fēēd·thē
littl~e~·cat.

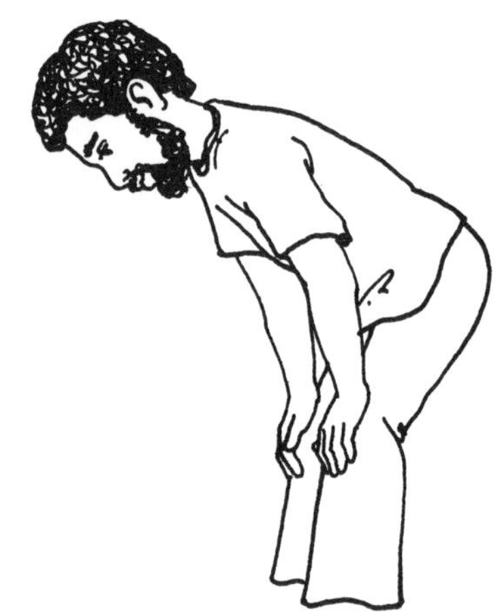

that·man·has
fat·fēēt.

shē·has·fun
in·thē·rāin.

mack·sat
on·a·rock.

Name ______________________________

Trace the words on the page. The words tell you things you *might* find in the picture. Look for those things in the picture. Copy the words for the things you find.

fin

rug

man

hat

ham

hand

sand

sun

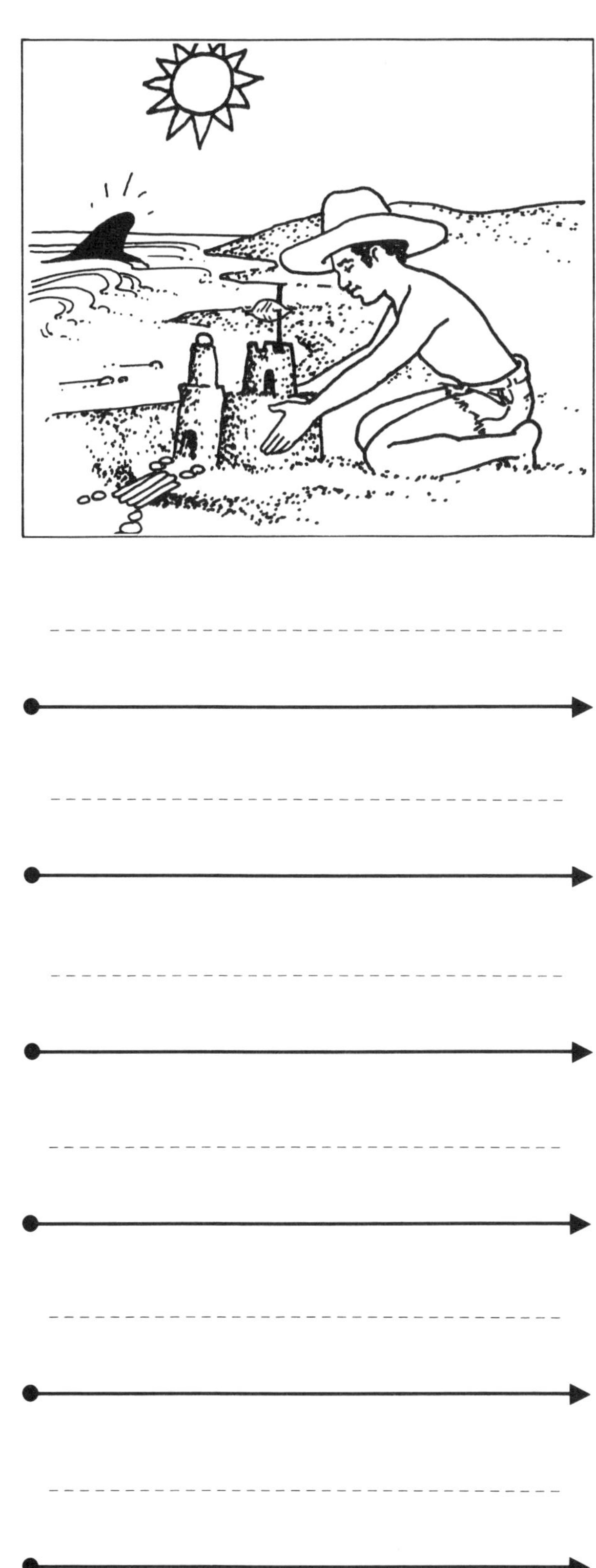

Name ________________________________ **Lesson 86**

Copy the *www* in each dotted-line box at the bottom of the page. Then cut out the dotted-line boxes. Paste one under each picture whose name begins with *www*.

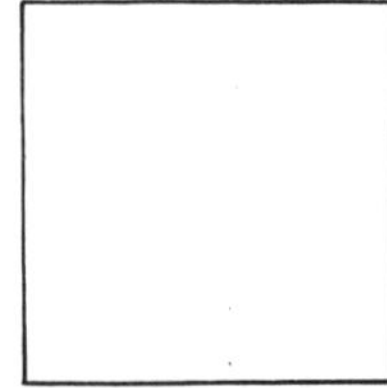

Look at each picture and read the sentences below it. Circle the sentence that tells about the picture. When you finish, color all the pictures.

shē has māil.

shē has a lock.

thē rug is his.

thē sock is his.

it is on a hat.

it is on a hut.

ron is in thē sun.

ron is in thē mud.

Name ____________________

Cut out the words at the bottom of the page. Paste each word in the box next to the picture it matches. Then copy the words.

Copy each sentence next to the picture it matches. Then color the pictures.

shē has a cat.

shē has a fan.

shē has a rug.

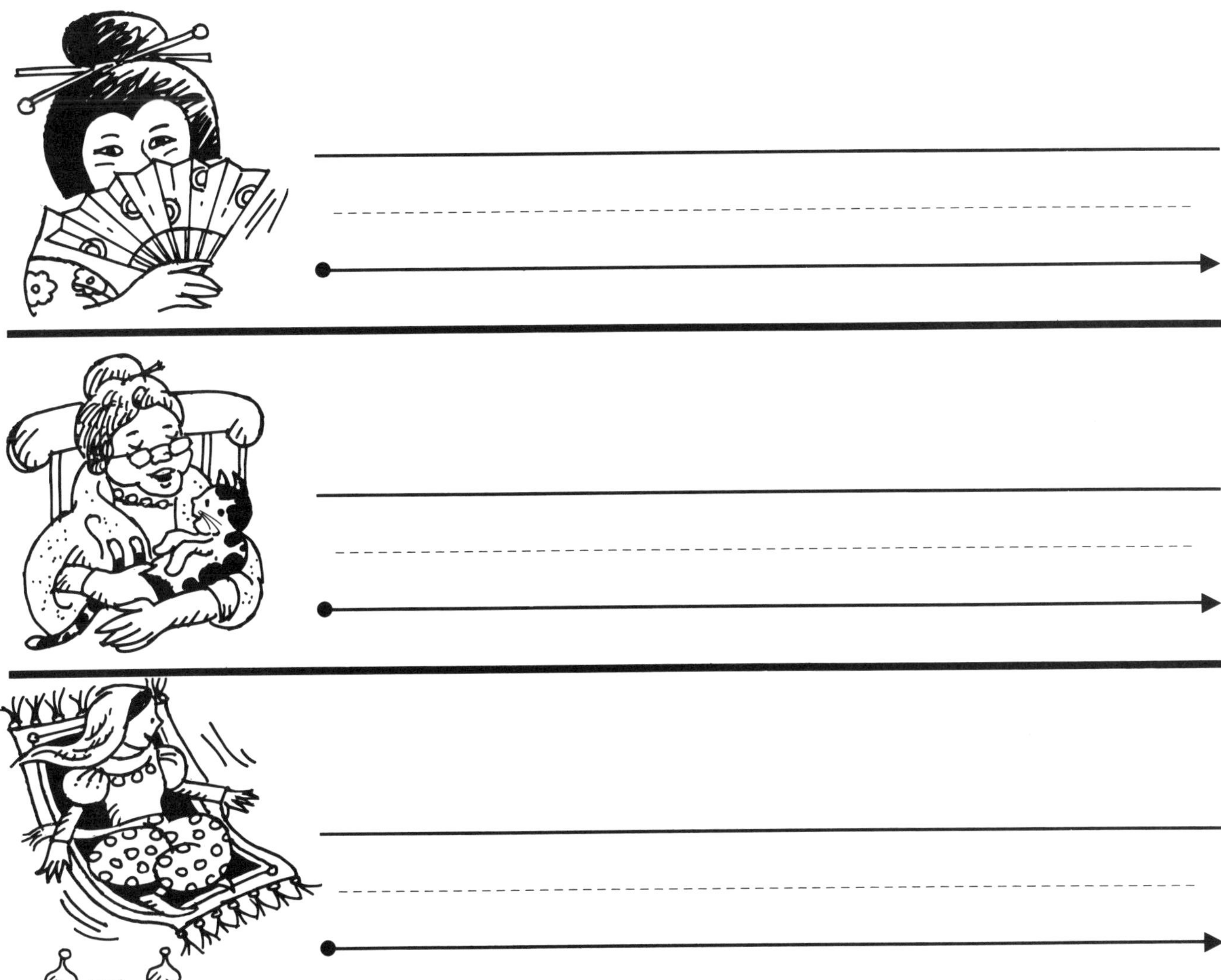

Name ____________________ Lesson 90

Write *shshsh* under each picture whose name begins with *shshsh*. When you finish, color the pictures you wrote *shshsh* under.

sh

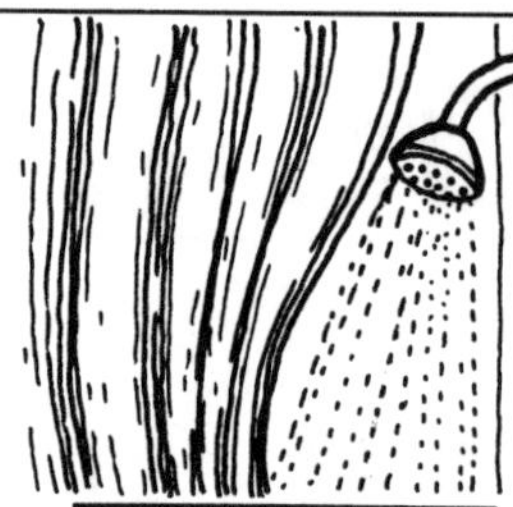

7

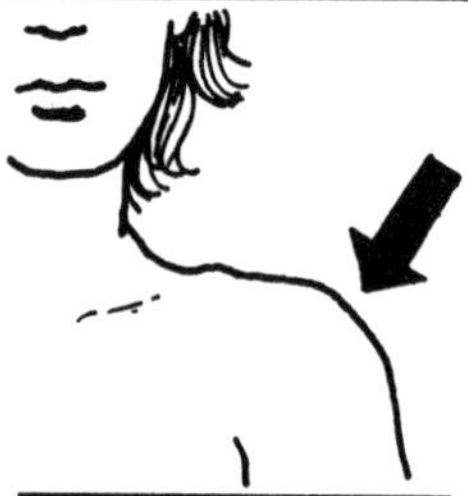

Name ____

Trace the words on the page. The words tell you things you *might* find in the picture. Look for those things in the picture. Copy the words for the things you find.

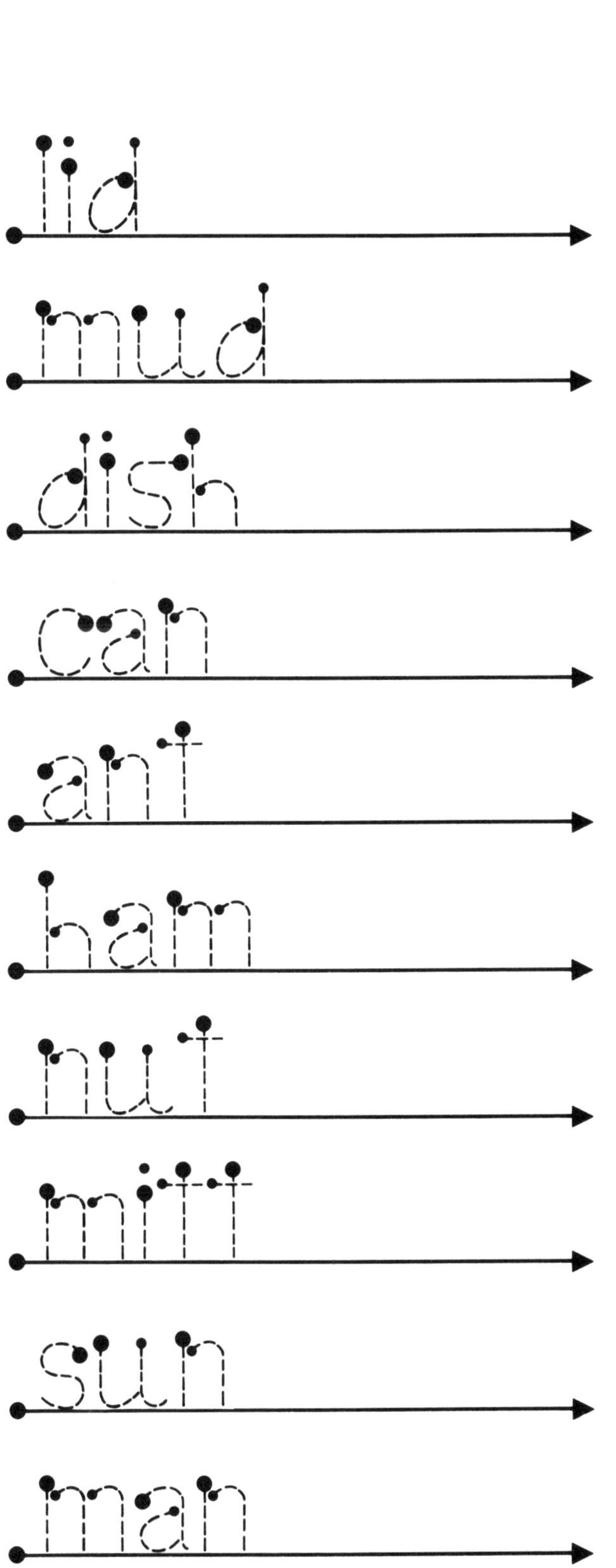

lid
mud
dish
can
ant
ham
nut
mitt
sun
man

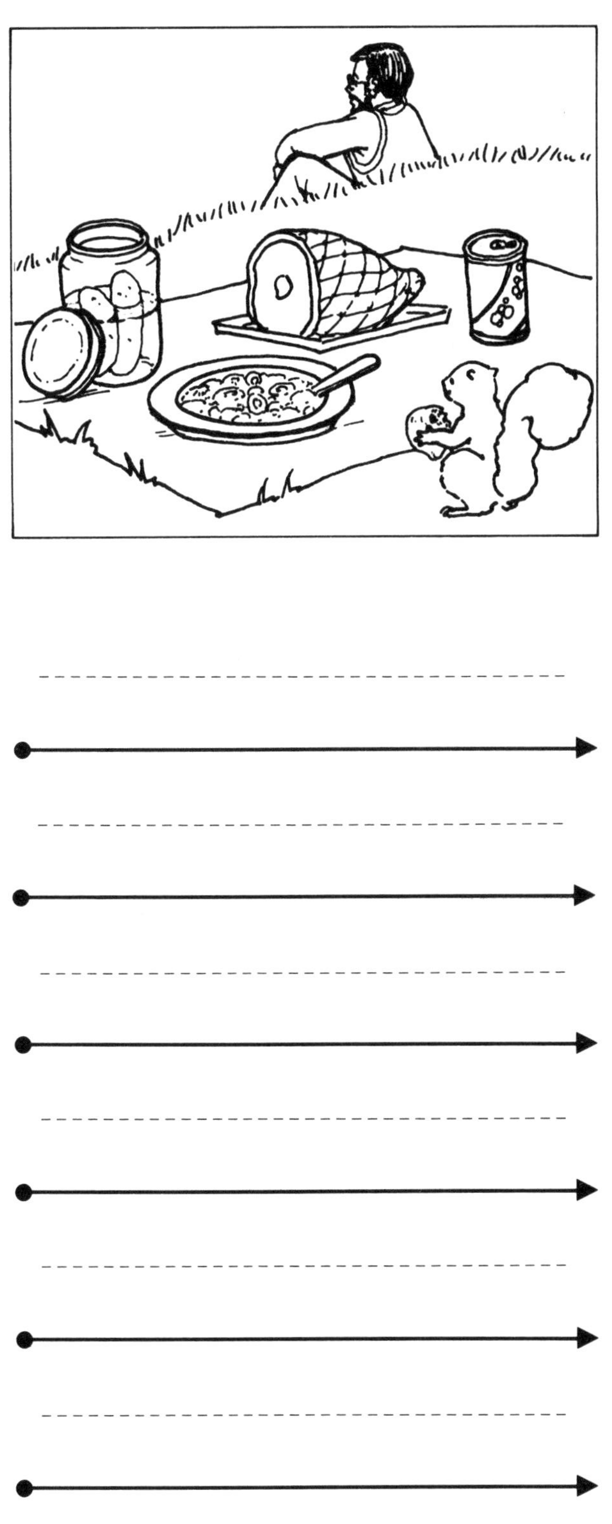

Name ____________________ Lesson 92

These groups of words don't make sense because they're not in the right order. Put the words in order. Write them in the boxes. Then finish the pictures so they show what the words say.

Name ____________________

There's a part missing from each picture on this page. Read the sentences to find out what parts are missing. Draw in the missing parts. Then color all the pictures.

that cat has
little ears.

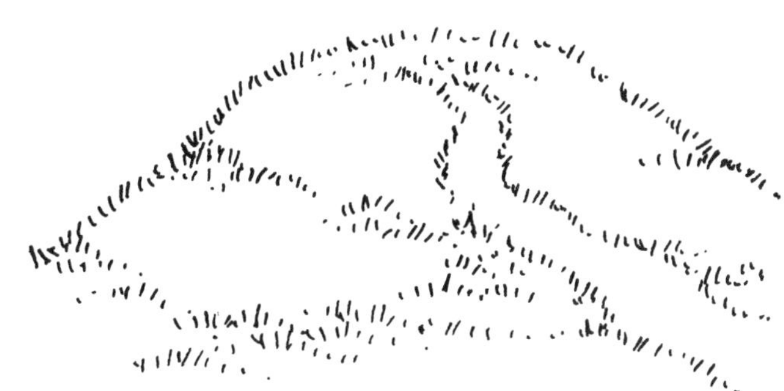

thē hut is on
thē hill.

dan got a fish.

thē ant runs
on a dish.

Name ______________________________

Make each word match the picture next to it. Choose the correct letter from the box and write it in the blank.

w f

___in

___in

n h

___ut

___ut

h s

___and

___and

s l r

___ock

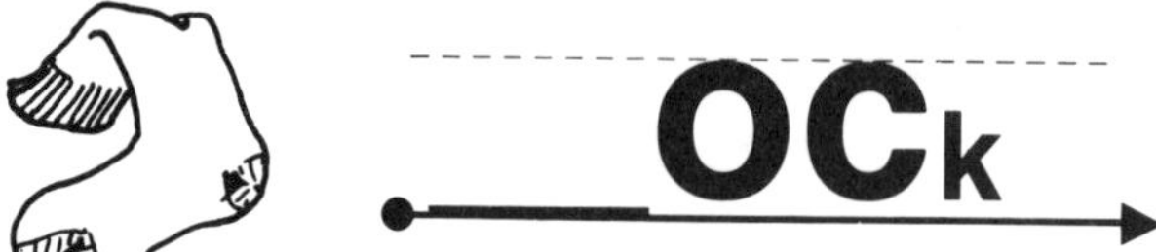

___ock

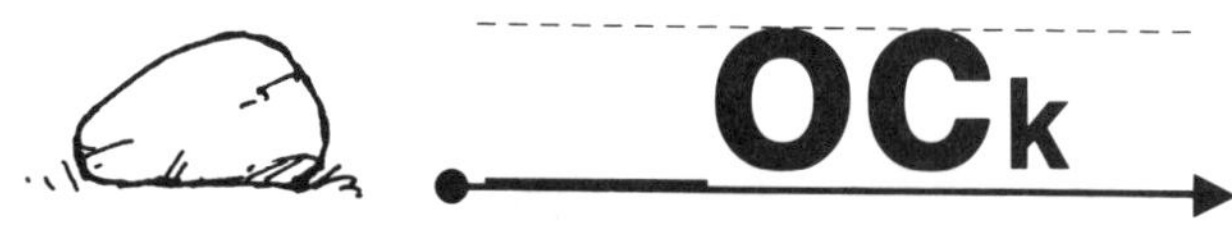

___ock

s sh b

___ack

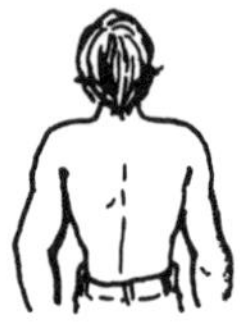

___ack

___ack

Copy each sentence next to the picture it matches. Then color the pictures.

shē has a mitt.

it has a lid.

hē has a hat.

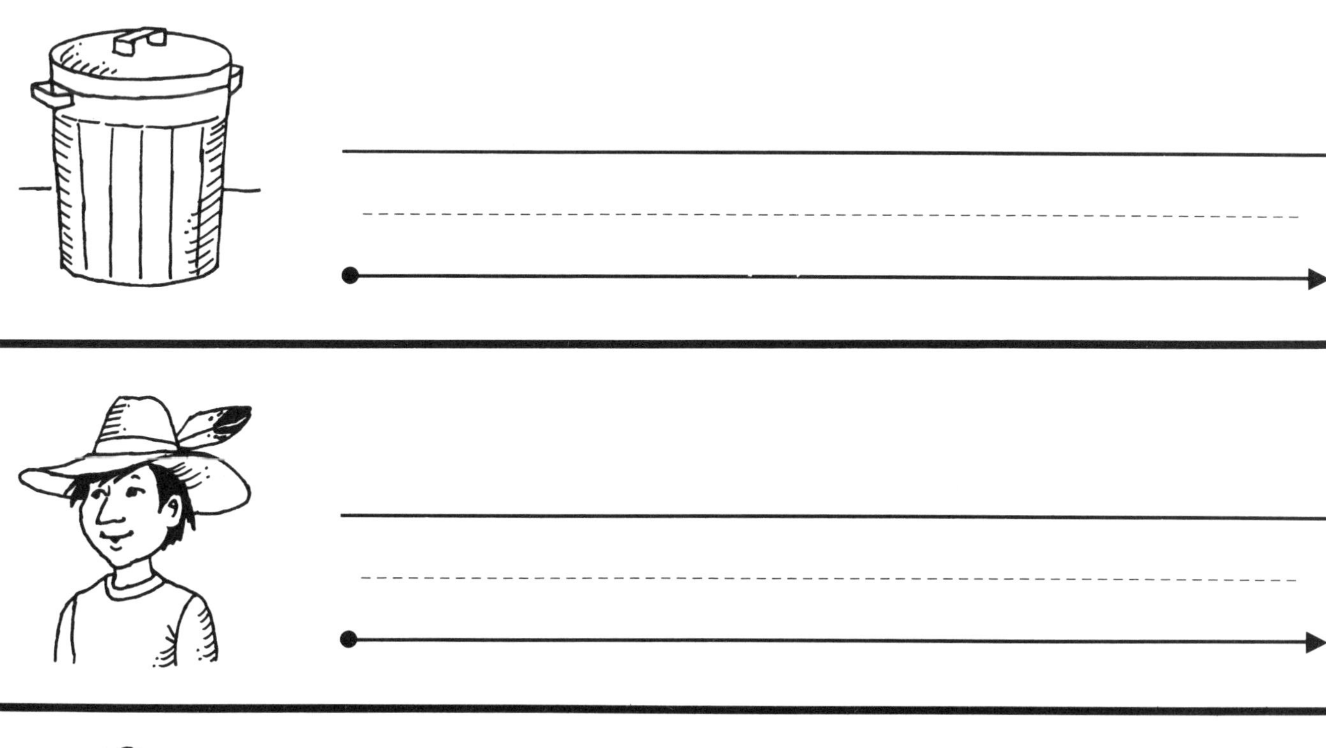

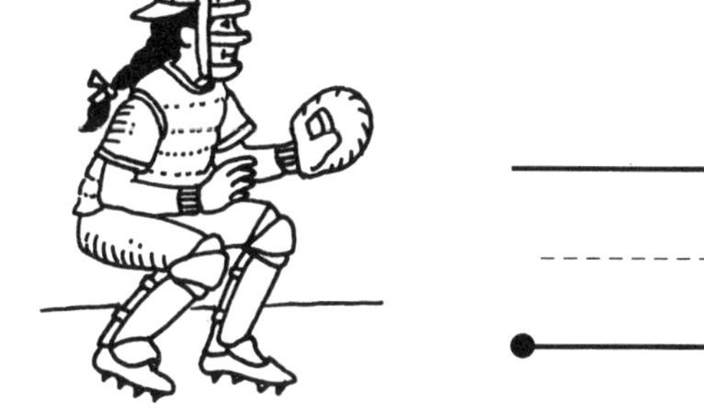

Name ______________________________ Lesson 96

Look at each picture and read the sentences below it. Circle the sentence that tells about the picture. When you finish, color all the pictures.

shē hēars a cow.

shē hēars a fish.

shē hit a cow.

a man has nō ēars.

a man has ēars.

a cat has ēars.

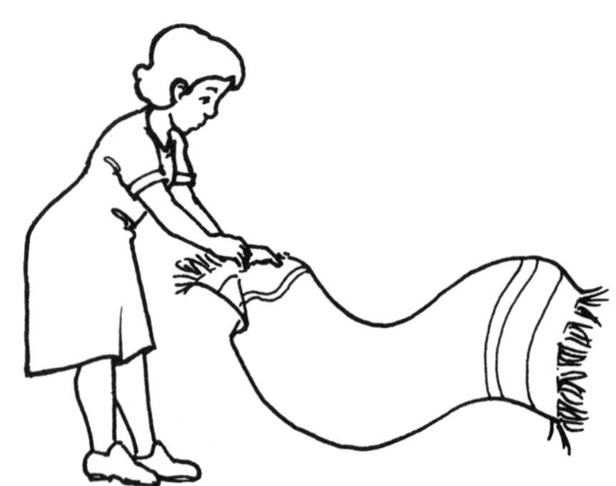

shē got a ham.

shē got a rug.

shē got a nut.

a man has a ram.

a man has a hat.

a man has a cat.

Name ____________________

Read the word on the arrow at the beginning of each row of letters. That word is hidden in the row of letters. Find the hidden words and circle them. Then draw a picture of the last word—*cow.*

win →	w	i	n	l	o	w	i	r	w
sun →	s	g	s	u	n	s	r	u	s
lid →	g	l	i	d	d	l	i	u	b
got →	n	m	t	g	i	g	o	t	o
did →	i	d	c	d	i	d	a	u	i
mom →	k	m	o	ē	t	h	m	o	m
digs →	s	g	c	d	i	g	s	t	i
cow →	o	a	w	o	c	o	w	c	r

Unscramble each set of words to make a sentence. The first word in each sentence is started for you. When you finish, color the picture.

sad. sam is

has a hut. dan

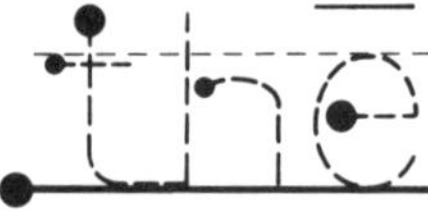

fat. thē is ram

thē is hot. sun

thē

Name ______________________________

There's a part missing from each picture on this page. Read the sentences to find out what parts are missing. Draw in the missing parts. Then color all the pictures.

this man has
a hat on.

a shack is
near the lake.

the cat sat
on the gate.

the cow licks
the sad man.

Name ____________________ Lesson 100

Make each word match the picture next to it. Choose the correct letter from the box and write it in the blank.

Name ______________________ Lesson 101

Copy each sentence next to the picture it matches. Then color the pictures.

a cat is fat.

a ram is fat.

a rat is not fat.

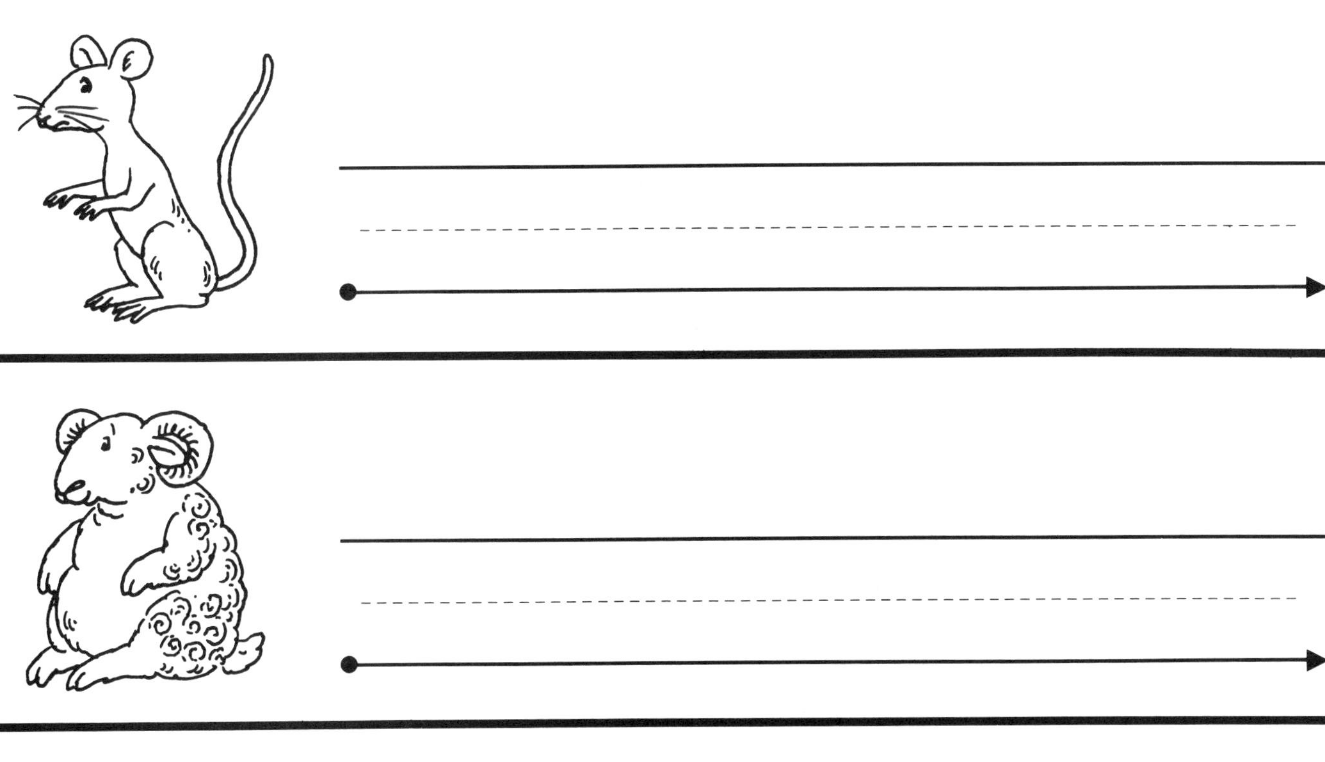

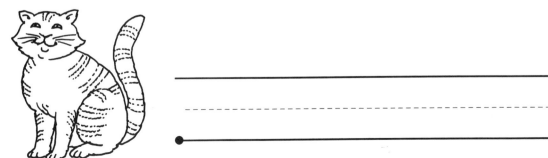

Name ____________________ Lesson 102

Copy the *k* in each dotted-line box at the bottom of the page. Then cut out the dotted-line boxes. Paste one under each picture whose name begins with *k*.

k

Make the sentences match the pictures. Circle the right word to finish each sentence. When you finish, color the pictures.

1. mom has a ______

fish. sack. wish.

2. hit thē ______

sāil. cat. nāil.

3. it is a hot ______

rock. shot. dish.

4. wē can ______

rock. rēad. ēat.

5. sit on thē ______

nut. gāme. gāte.

6. thē hat is on a ______

hand. sēat. rat.

Name ______________________________ Lesson 104

Unscramble each set of letters to make a word. Write the word on the line. The first letter of each word is started for you. When you finish, draw a picture of the word at the bottom of the page. Color your picture.

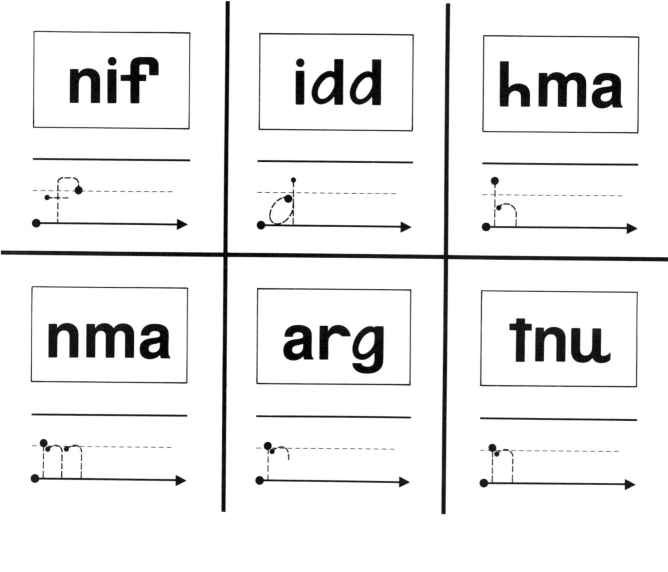

nif

idd

hma

nma

arg

tnu

Name ______________________________

Unscramble each set of words to make a sentence. The first word in each sentence is started for you. When you finish, color the picture.

man thē is ōld.

the

cow thē fat. is

the

thē hat sōld. was

the

is mad. thē man

the

There's a part missing from each picture on this page. Read the sentences to find out what parts are missing. Draw in the missing parts. Then color all the pictures.

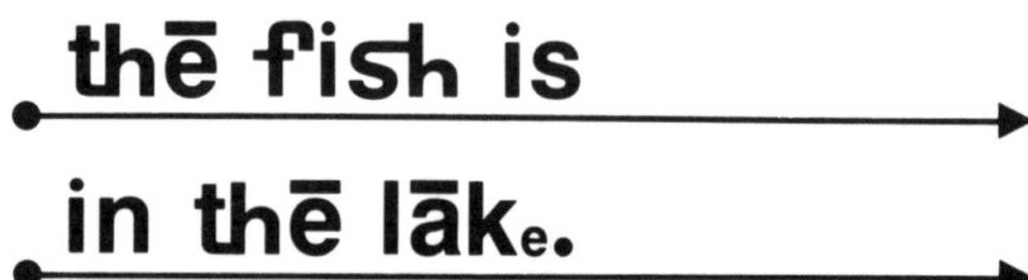

thē fish is
in thē lāke.

dan has an ant
on his nōse.

hē gāve his
mom a cāke.

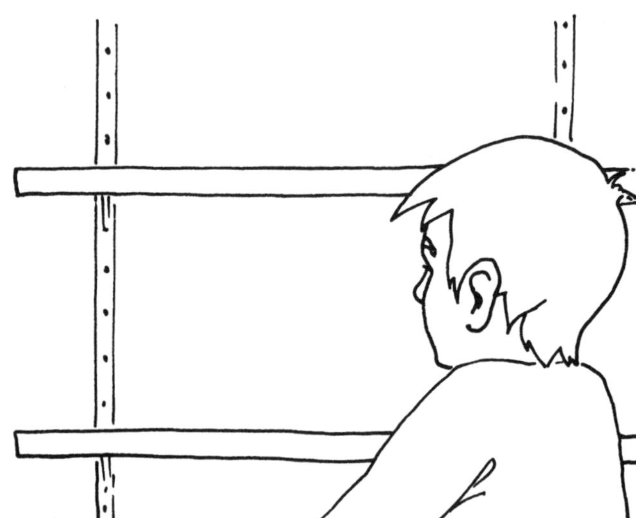

sam has lots
of hats.

Name ____________________

Make each word match the picture next to it. Choose the correct letter from the box and write it in the blank.

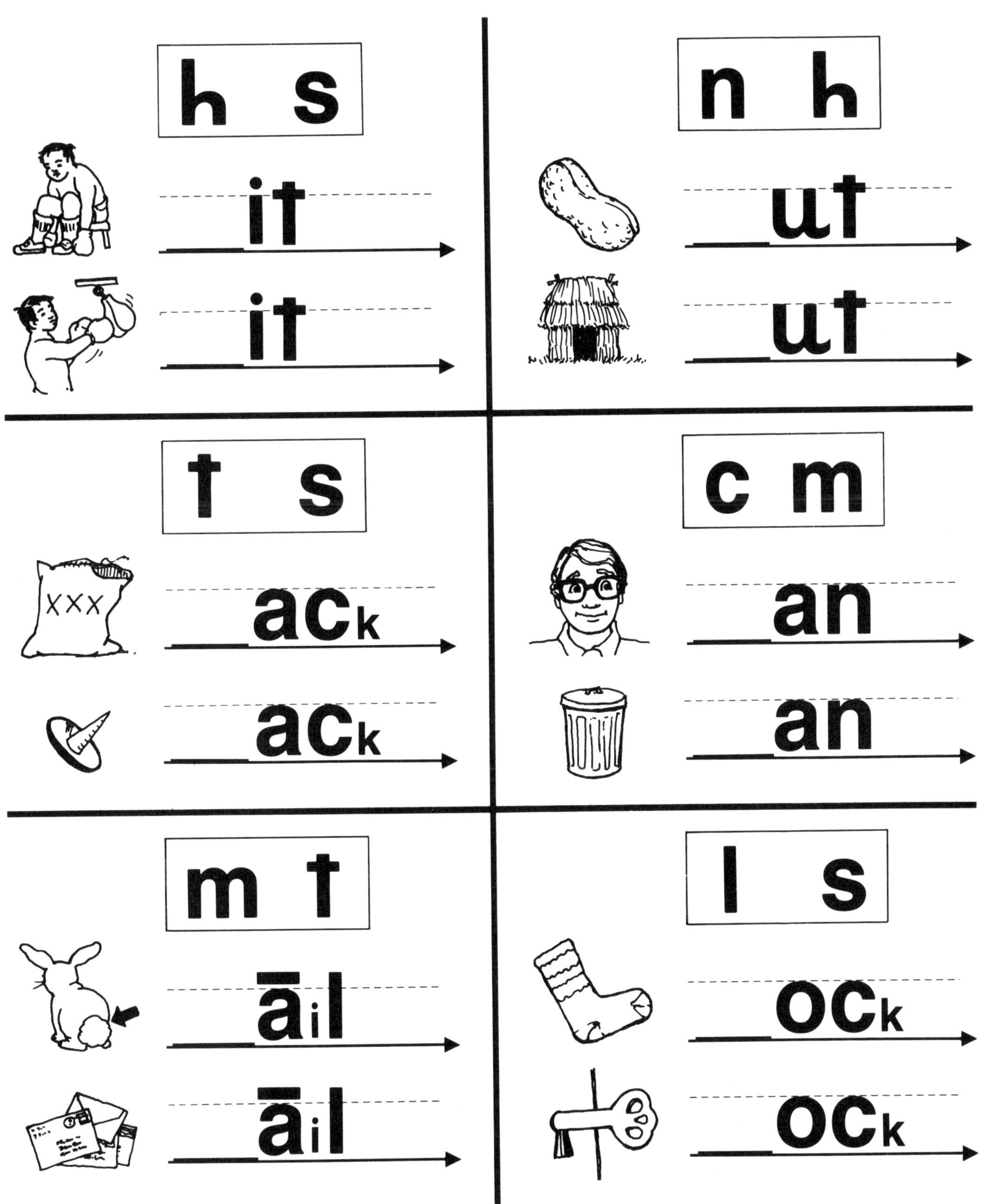

Name ____________________ Lesson 108

Copy the word that goes with each picture. Then color all the pictures.

can

cow

fan

fat

hut

hug

mud

mom

hat

has

sin

sun

Name ______________________________

Read the sentences. Circle *yes* if a sentence is right or *no* if a sentence is not right. When you finish all the sentences, color the picture.

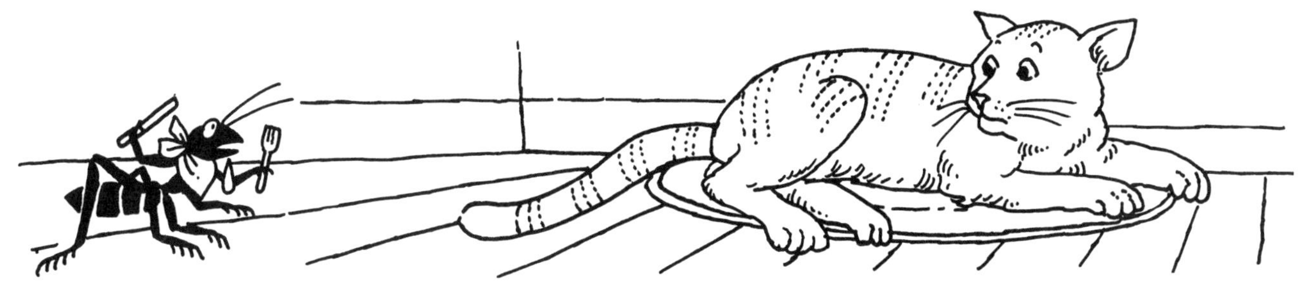

1. an ant can ēat a cat. •yes •nō
2. a cow has a tail. •yes •nō
3. ham is mēat. •yes •nō
4. a man can run. •yes •nō
5. a fish has fēēt. •yes •nō
6. rats can rēad. •yes •nō
7. a dish can kiss. •yes •nō
8. a cat has ēars. •yes •nō
9. a cop can hōld a mop. •yes •nō

Name ______________________________

Unscramble each set of letters to make a word. Write the word on the line. The first letter of each word is started for you. When you finish, draw a picture of the word at the bottom of the page. Color your picture.

niw

w

snu

s

guh

h

dno

n

fna

f

ishw

w

Name ______________________________ Lesson 111

Unscramble each set of words to make a sentence. The first word in each sentence is started for you. When you finish, color the picture.

cop. a mom is

has dog. a shē

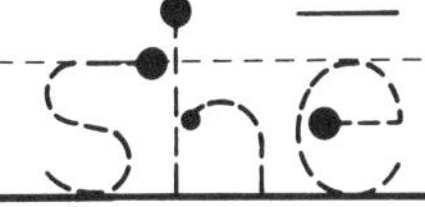

sand. in sits dan

for he fun. digs

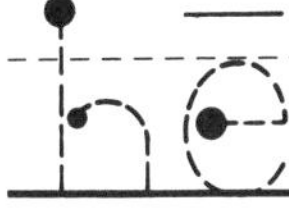

Name ____ Lesson 112

Cut out the words at the bottom of the page. Paste each word at the end of the sentence it finishes.

I have to fēēd thē  .

the ship has a  .

thē kitten sat on his 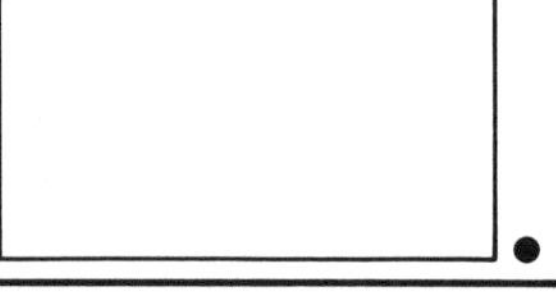 .

hē hēars with his  .

she māde a ____________ .

tāil	sāil	cāke	cats	ēars

Name ____ Lesson 113

Make each word match the picture next to it. Choose the correct letter from the box and write it in the blank.

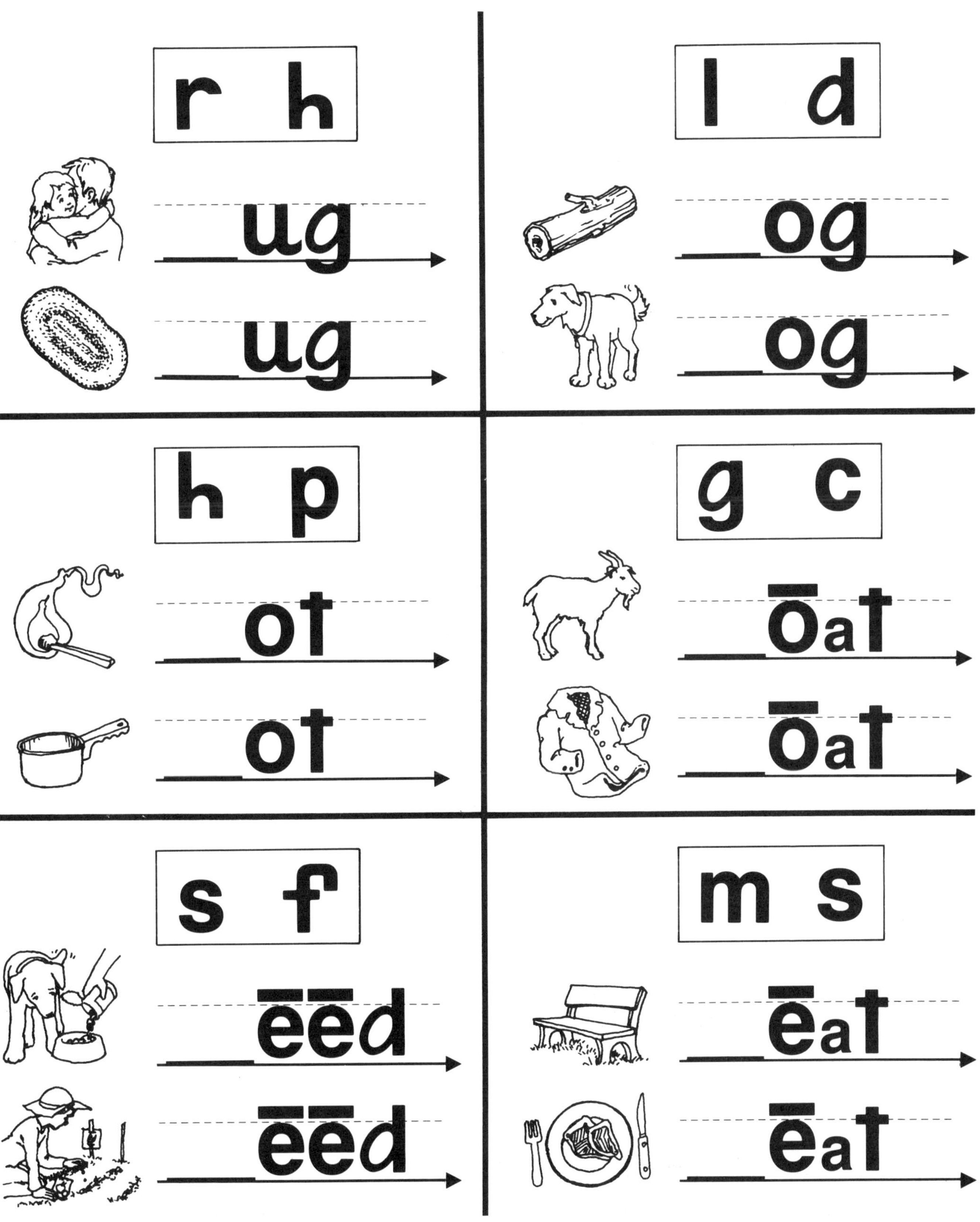

Look at each picture and read the sentences below it. Circle the sentence that tells about the picture. When you finish, color all the pictures.

shē āte a fish.

shē āte mēat.

shē āte a dish.

this dog is fat.

this dog is mēan.

this dog is sad.

kick thē top.

kick thē car.

kick thē can.

wē have a cōat.

wē have a gōat.

wē have a gāte.

Name ______________________________

Unscramble each set of letters to make a word. Write the word on the line. When you finish, draw a picture of the word at the bottom of the page. Color your picture.

ufn

ild

nsi

dmu

nar

uht

mmo

Name ______________________________

Copy each sentence next to the picture it matches. Then color the pictures.

sēē thē top gō.

sēē thē dog gō.

sēē thē ship gō.

Name ______________________________

There's a part missing from each picture on this page. Read the sentences to find out what parts are missing. Draw in the missing parts. Then color all the pictures.

a kitten is on top of thē car.

thē ship has a sāil.

thē cop has a sock in his hand.

thē girl has an ōld gōat.

Name ______________________ **Lesson 118**

Write *p* under each picture whose name begins with *p*. When you finish, color the pictures you wrote *p* under.

p

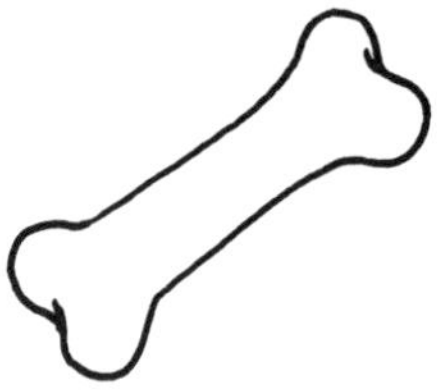

Name ______________________________ Lesson 119

Make each word match the picture next to it. Choose the correct letter from the box and write it in the blank.

Name ____________________ Lesson 120

Read the sentences. Circle *yes* if a sentence is right or *no* if a sentence is not right. When you finish all the sentences, color the picture.

1. a gōat can bē ōld. → •yes •nō
2. a man can ēat a nut. → •yes •nō
3. rocks have ēars. → •yes •nō
4. socks have tēēth. → •yes •nō
5. rāin will gō down. → •yes •nō
6. a man can shāve. → •yes •nō
7. a mop can hug. → •yes •nō
8. a gāte can have a lock. → •yes •nō
9. a kitten has a nōse. → •yes •nō

Name ______________________________

Cut out the words at the bottom of the page. Paste each word at the end of the sentence it finishes.

the cows āte [ ].

his tēam will win the [ ].

pigs can not [ ].

the kitten is [ ].

the girl can sēē [ ].

ōats	far	gāme	little	rēad

Name ______________________________ Lesson 122

Finish each sentence with a word from the bottom of the page. Then write those words in the crossword puzzle. Match the number of the sentence with the number in the puzzle. Some words will go across and some will go down.

1. fēēd the ______.

2. gō up to the ______.

3. dan ______.

4. mom will ēat ______.

5. socks fit on ______.

nuts

cows

top

runs

fēēt

Name ______________________________

Write *ch* under each picture whose name begins with *ch*. When you finish, color the pictures you wrote *ch* under.

ch

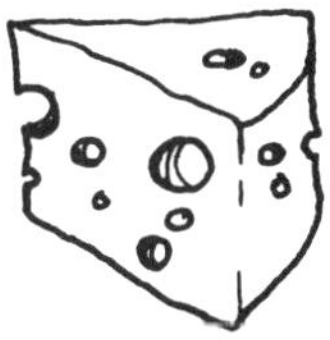

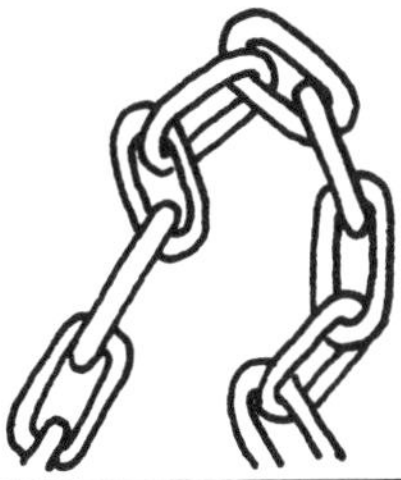

Name ______________________________ Lesson 124

Unscramble each set of words to make a sentence. The first word in each sentence is started for you. When you finish, color the picture.

sal mop. has a

she with sam. is

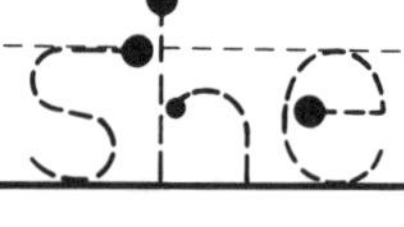

hug I cat. the

I

mitt. the dan wins

dan

Name ______________________________ Lesson 125

Cut out the words at the bottom of the page. Paste each word at the end of the sentence it finishes.

hē āte the ☐.

the dog had a little ☐.

a car cāme down the ☐.

the duck will get ☐.

shē will fish in the ☐.

rōad	wet	nōse	lāke	chips

Name ______________________________ Lesson 126

Trace the words on the page. The words tell you things you *might* find in the picture. Look for those things in the picture. Copy the words for the things you find.

hats

guns

kitten

fog

mop

dog

top

teeth

kiss

log

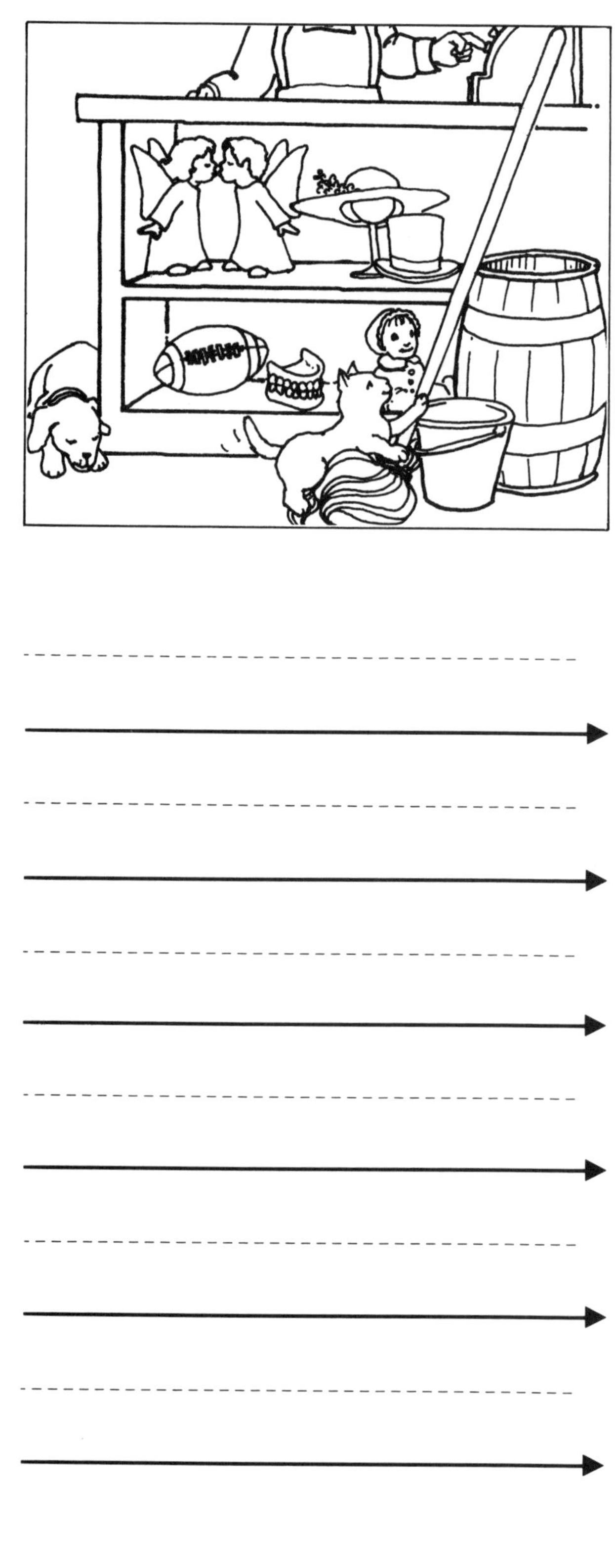

Read the sentences. Circle *yes* if a sentence is right or *no* if a sentence is not right. When you finish all the sentences, color the picture.

1. cars can gō on rōads. •yes •nō
2. lākes are wet. •yes •nō
3. a rug has a hand. •yes •nō
4. a dish has a tāil. •yes •nō
5. a kitten is a little cat. •yes •nō
6. a pig has a fin. •yes •nō
7. a nāil has ēars. •yes •nō
8. bugs can sit on logs. •yes •nō
9. fish can park cars. •yes •nō

Name ______________________________ Lesson 128

Read the story. Then write the correct word to finish each sentence. When you finish, draw a picture of the *hut* from the story.

I have a little hut.
it is on a hill. the
little hut is ōld. I
will pāint it red.

---

1. I have a little ________.
2. the hut is on a ________.
3. the little hut is ________.
4. I will pāint it ________.

the hut on a hill

Name ______________________________

Choose the right words to go with each picture. Write those words on the line. When you finish, color the pictures.

bed in pet

pet in bed

ten on can

can on ten

ship on men

men on ship

Name ______________________________________ Lesson 130

Copy each sentence next to the picture it matches. Then color the pictures.

the sun is hot.

the log is hot.

the pot is hot.

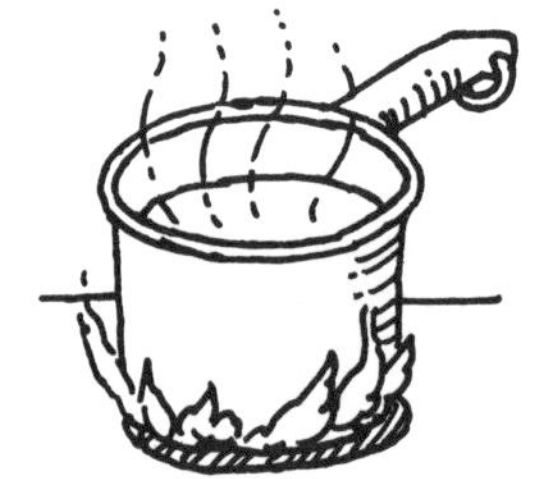

Name ____________________ Lesson 131

Write *b* under each picture whose name begins with *b*. When you finish, color the pictures you wrote *b* under.

b

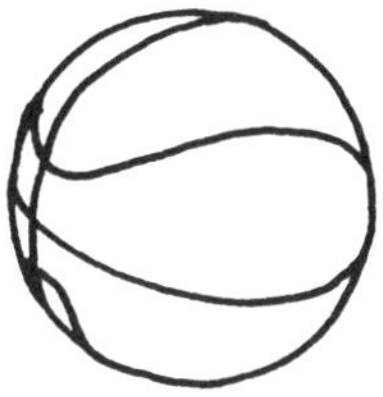

Name ____________________ Lesson 132

Finish each sentence with a word from the bottom of the page. Then write those words in the crossword puzzle. Match the number of the sentence with the number in the puzzle. Some words will go across and some will go down.

1. mom likes ________.

2. the dog ________.

3. ann is a ________.

4. the pot has a ________.

5. I run up the ________.

girl

digs

lid

hill

hats

Name ______________________________

Read the sentences. Circle *yes* if a sentence is right or *no* if a sentence is not right. When you finish all the sentences, color the picture.

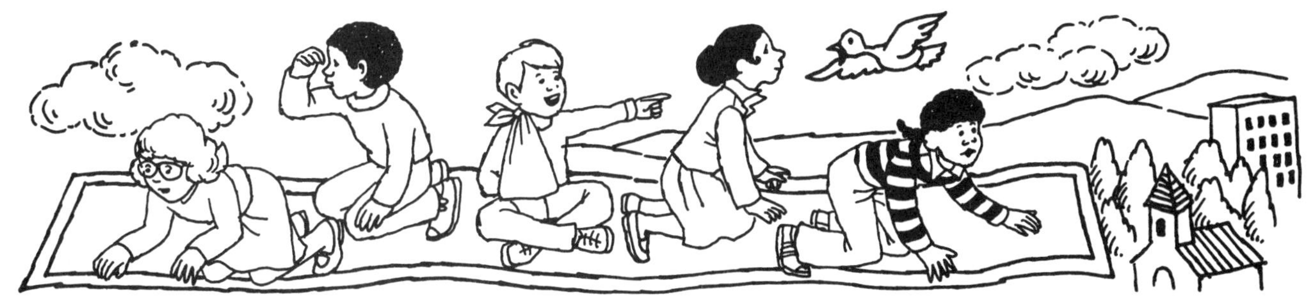

1. wē can sit on a rug. ________ •yes •nō

2. the sun is hot. ________ •yes •nō

3. bugs līke to shop. ________ •yes •nō

4. rāin can bē cōld. ________ •yes •nō

5. a pot can have a lid. ________ •yes •nō

6. a lock can hēar. ________ •yes •nō

7. cows can kick. ________ •yes •nō

8. a pig has a nōse. ________ •yes •nō

9. rocks nēēd slēēp. ________ •yes •nō

Name ______________________________ Lesson 134

Copy the word that goes with each picture. Then color all the pictures.

Name ______________________________ Lesson 135

Read the story. Then write the correct word to finish each sentence. When you finish, draw a picture of *Sam* and *Dan* from the story.

sam is a man. his cat is dan. sam slēēps in a bed. his cat slēēps on a rug.

---

1. sam is a ______.
2. dan is a ______.
3. sam slēēps in a ______.
4. dan slēēps on a ______.

sam and dan

Name ______________________________ Lesson 136

Cut out the words at the bottom of the page. Paste each word in the box next to the picture it matches. Then copy the words.

teeth	feet	cow
fish	corn	arm

Name ____________________

Copy the word that goes with each picture. Then color all the pictures.

wāving
dīving

cut
bug

hill
him

can
car

pond
pot

top
cop

Name ____________________

Choose the right words to go with each picture. Write those words on the line. When you finish, color the pictures.

corn in cops

cops in corn

sam hugs ram

ram hugs sam

dish on fish

fish on dish

Name ____________________

Read the story and the sentences below it. Circle *yes* if a sentence is right. Circle *no* if a sentence is wrong
When you finish, color the picture.

ann and al are little bugs. they live in a hōle in a log. they rēad and ēat in the hōle. they slēēp on ōld socks.

1. ann is a little bug. •yes •nō

2. al is a big bug. •yes •nō

3. they live in a hōle. •yes •nō

4. the hōle is in a hut. •yes •nō

5. ann and al rēad and ēat. •yes •nō

6. they slēēp on ōld rocks. •yes •nō

Name ____________________

Finish each sentence with a word from the bottom of the page. Then write those words in the crossword puzzle. Match the number of the sentence with the number in the puzzle. Some words will go across and some will go down.

1. they slēēp in ________.
2. the car is ________.
3. do not hit his ________.
4. cows live on ________.
5. fish live in ________.

hand
ponds
beds
farms
red

1.
2.
3.
4.
5.

Name ____ Lesson 141

Trace the words on the page. The words tell you things you *might* find in the picture. Look for those things in the picture. Copy the words for the things you find.

tub

pig

cow

rabbit

bug

bōy

pot

pond

girl

shēēp

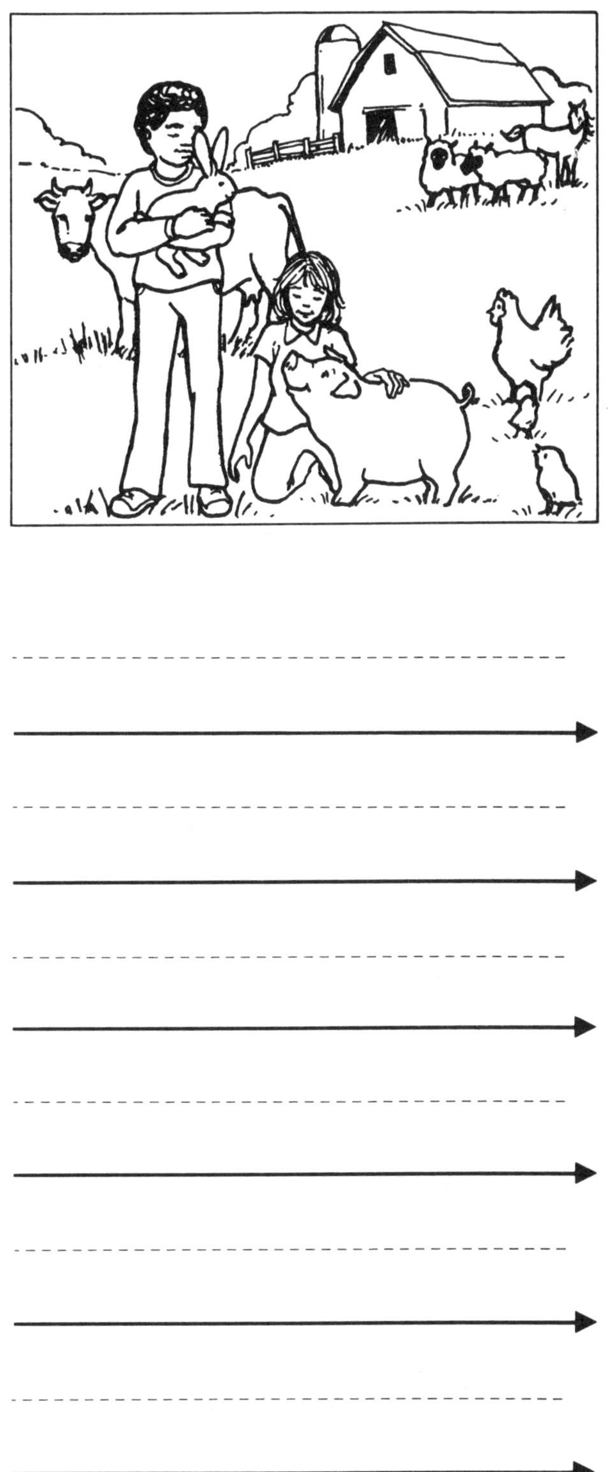

Name ________________________________

Read the story. Then write the correct word to finish each sentence. When you finish, draw a picture of *Mack* and *Sal* from the story.

mack and sal are pigs.
they live on a farm.
they sit in the mud.
they ēat lots of corn.

---

1. mack and sal are ________.
2. they live on a ________.
3. they sit in the ________.
4. they eat lots of ________.

mack and sal

Name ______________________________

Cut out the faces at the bottom of the page. Paste each face on the head next to the story it goes with.

shē kicks the gāte. →

shē hits her pet pig. →

the girl is mēan. →

---

the bōy is sad. →

hē can not fīnd his dog. →

sēē the tēar. →

---

mȳ brother līkes cats. →

hē got a little kitten. →

wow. →

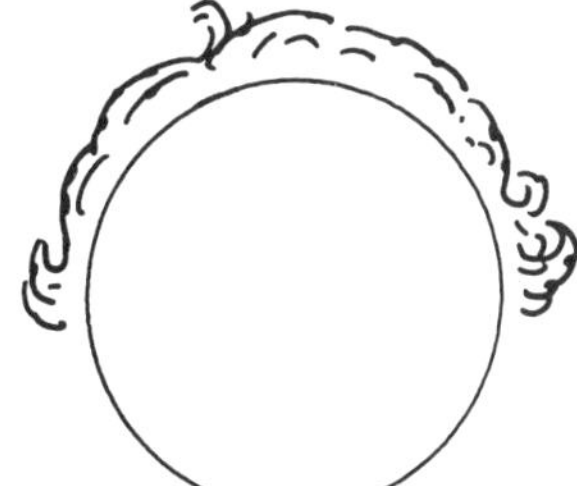

Ī āte lots of nuts. →

now Ī fēēl sick. →

Ī nēēd to slēēp. →

Name ________________________________ Lesson 144

Finish each sentence with a word from the bottom of the page. Then write those words in the crossword puzzle. Match the number of the sentence with the number in the puzzle. Some words will go across and some will go down.

1. pigs ēat ________.

2. hop līke a ________.

3. pāint the ________.

4. wē walk on ________.

5. his tēam ________.

corn
barn
rugs
frog
wins

1.
2.
3.
4.
5.

Name ____________________ Lesson 145

Read the story and the sentences below it. Circle *yes* if a sentence is right. Circle *no* if a sentence is wrong. When you finish, color the picture.

a bug lived on a leaf. a rabbit came to eat the leaf. "nō," said the bug, "I love this leaf." sō thē bug āte the leaf.

1. a rabbit lived on a bug. •yes •nō

2. a bug lived on a leaf. •yes •nō

3. the rabbit came to eat. •yes •nō

4. the bug āte the rabbit. •yes •nō

5. the rabbit āte the leaf. •yes •nō

Name ______________________________ Lesson 146

Unscramble each set of words to make a sentence. The first word in each sentence is started for you. When you finish, color the picture.

a girl digging. is

a

the cōld. is bōy

the

brother. her hē is

hē

sēē a they rabbit.

they

Name ______________________________ Lesson 147

Cut out the words at the bottom of the page. Paste each word in the box next to the picture it matches. Then copy the words.

dish	dēēr	pig
brush	ship	girl

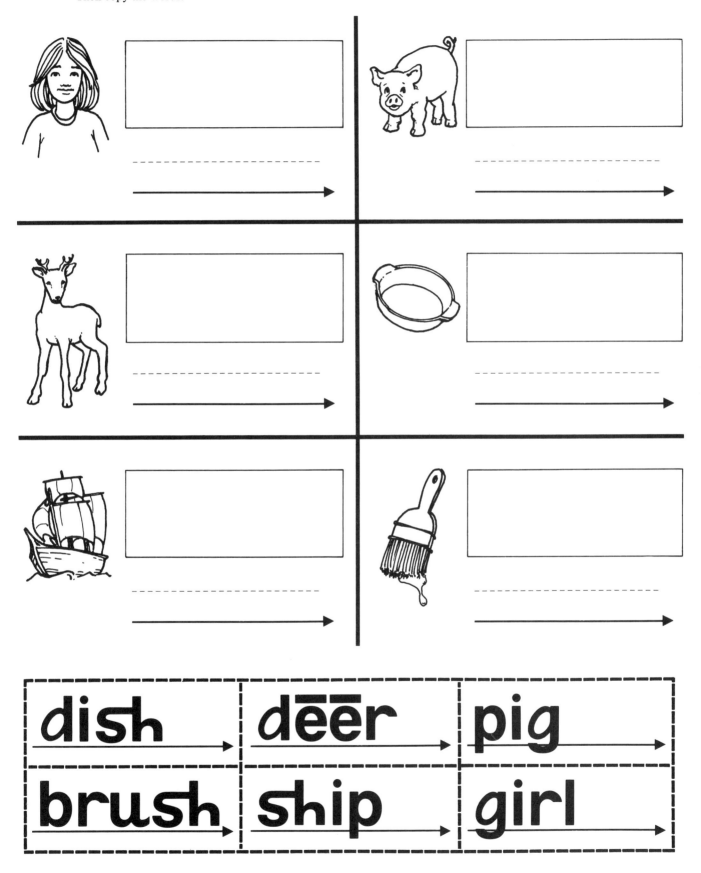

Name ____ **Lesson 148**

Cut out the pictures at the bottom of the page. Paste each picture in the box next to the sentence it goes with. When you finish, color the pictures.

1. let's pāint the room red. → [ ]

2. I must dig a hōle. → [ ]

3. I līke to rēad. → [ ]

4. I have a sōre leg. → [ ]

5. I love to gō shopping. → [ ]

Read the sentences. Circle *yes* if a sentence is right or *no* if a sentence is not right. When you finish all the sentences, color the picture.

1. a frog līkes to jump. •yes •nō
2. gōats slēēp in a pond. •yes •nō
3. a gun can swim. •yes •nō
4. cows live on farms. •yes •nō
5. a broom has ten ēars. •yes •nō
6. a lēaf can run. •yes •nō
7. a fox līkes shopping. •yes •nō
8. an ēagle can ēat. •yes •nō
9. it is dark in a cāve. •yes •nō

Name ____________________

Read the story. Then write the correct word to finish each sentence. When you finish, draw a picture of *Ann* and *Dan* from the story.

ann is a girl. her
brother is dan. they
like to ride the bus.
they gō to the park.

1. ann is a ____________.
2. dan is her ____________.
3. they ride the ____________.
4. they gō to the ____________.

ann and dan

Unscramble each set of letters to make a word. Write the word on the line. When you finish, draw a picture of the word at the bottom of the page. Color your picture.

dre

gol

bxo

gip

ocp

lōd

ugb

Name ________________________________

Cut out the faces at the bottom of the page. Paste each face on the head next to the story it goes with.

hē māde some cākes.
a gōat āte the cākes.
hē is mad.

shē went shopping.
shē walked a lot.
now shē must slēēp.

I fell down.
I have a sōre arm.
I am sad.

I am rīding a bīke.
I līke to rīde a bīke.
I am having fun.

Copy the word that goes with each picture. Then color all the pictures.

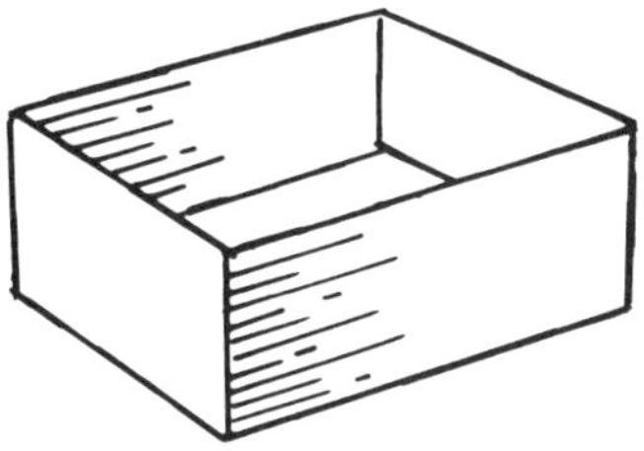

box
bōy

bad
broom

mop
moon

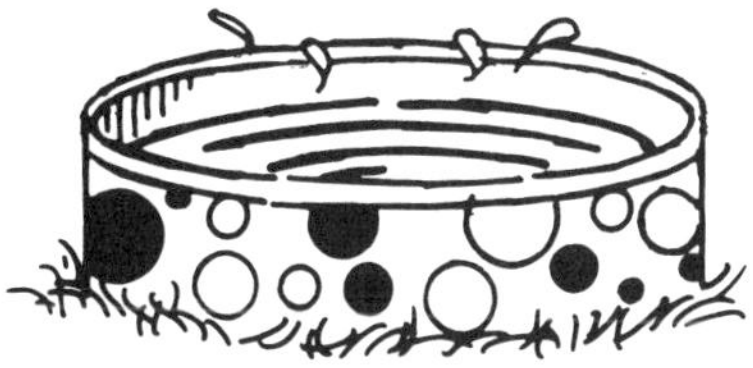

pool
pot

fox
for

run
room

Name ____________________

Finish each sentence with a word from the bottom of the page. Then write those words in the crossword puzzle. Match the number of the sentence with the number in the puzzle. Some words will go across and some will go down.

1. they ride in ________.

2. the room is ________.

3. fish eat ________.

4. the rabbit ________.

5. dogs are fine ________.

bugs

cars

dark

pets

jumps

1.

2.

3.

4.

5.

Read the story. Then write the correct word to finish each sentence. When you finish, draw a picture of the *digging dogs* from the story.

the dogs are digging.
they dig a hole in the
yard. dogs like to dig.
they dig for fun.

---

1. the dogs are ________.
2. a hole is in the ________.
3. dogs like to ________.
4. they dig for ________.

the digging dogs

Name ____________________

Cut out the pictures at the bottom of the page. Paste each picture in the box next to the sentence it goes with. When you finish, color the pictures.

1. I will ēat fish.

2. Where is the swimming pool?

3. I went to the moon.

4. mȳ cat līkes mē a lot.

5. mȳ hōme is on a farm.

Name ______________________________

Write *g* under each picture whose name begins with *g*. When you finish, color the pictures you wrote *g* under.

g

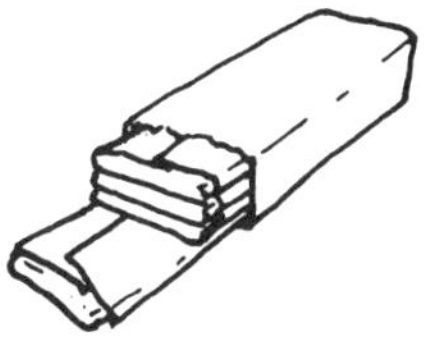

Name ______________________________________ **Lesson 158**

Read the story and the sentences below it. Circle *yes* if a sentence is right. Circle *no* if a sentence is wrong. When you finish, color the picture.

mack was a big cat.
hē sat on an ōld hat.
the hat was on mȳ
brother, pat.
a cat on a hat on pat.

1. mack was a little cat. •yes •nō
2. mack sat on a hat. •yes •nō
3. the hat was ōld. •yes •nō
4. the hat was on mack. •yes •nō
5. pat is mȳ brother. •yes •nō

Name ____________________

Copy the word that goes with each picture. Then color all the pictures.

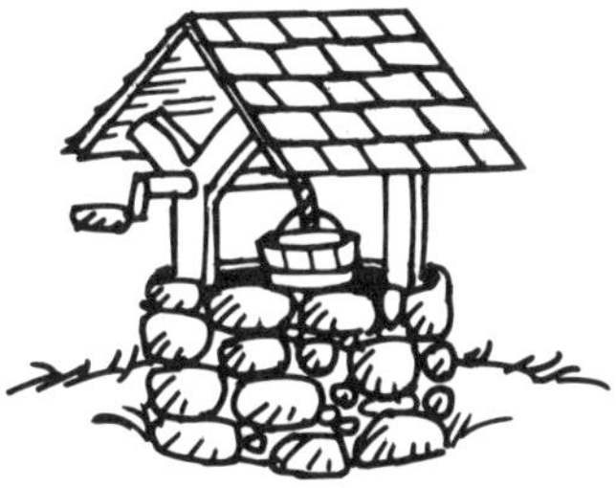

wē

well

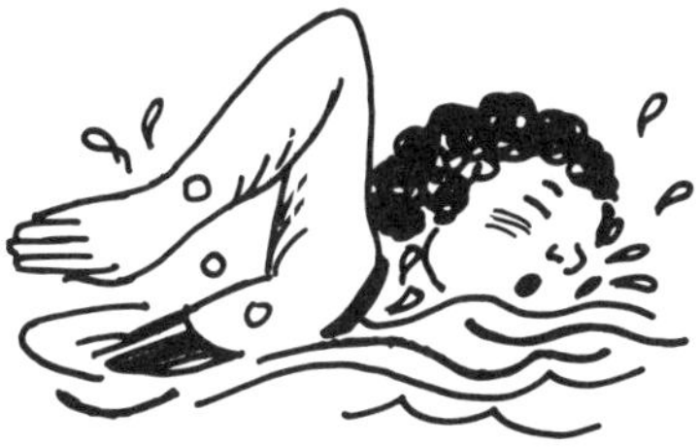

swim

slid

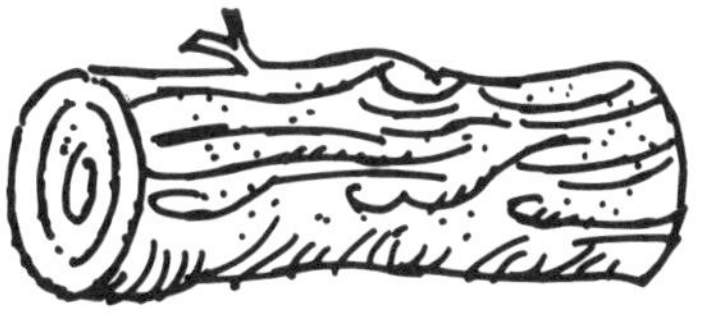

lot

log

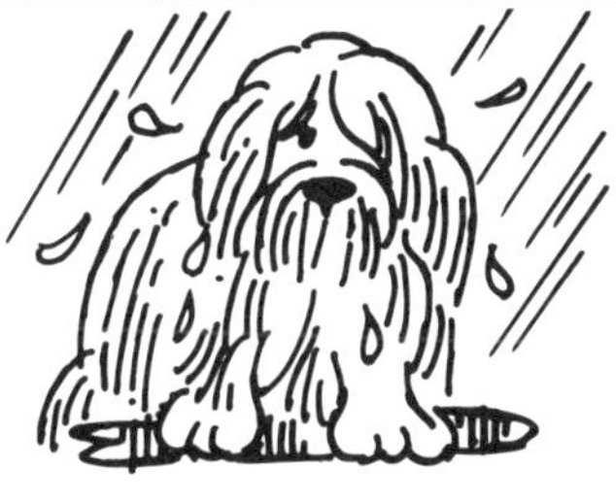

wet

went

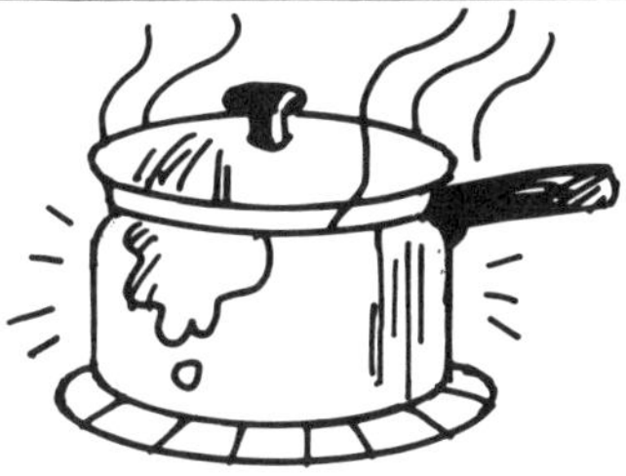

hot

how

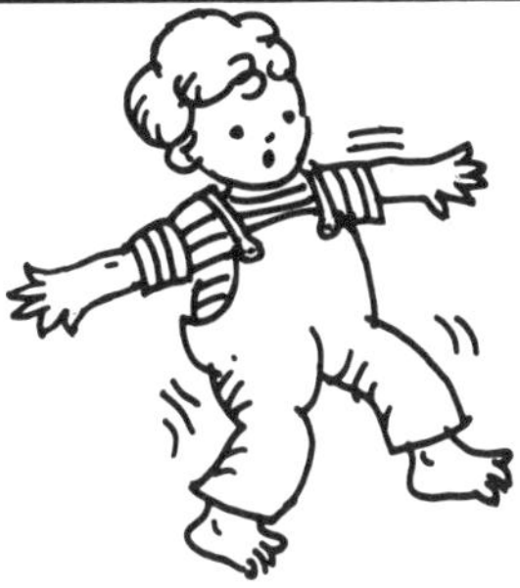

walk

wish

Cut out the faces at the bottom of the page. Paste each face on the head next to the story it goes with.

I had a red tōy.
mȳ dog brōke it.
now I am mad.

it was a hot day.
shē was walking fast.
shē was hot and wet.

there is a tīger.
will it bīte mē?
I will run awāy.

ann is gōing to the park.
shē will have fun.
look at ann smīle.

Answer Key

Lesson 1
11 stars: 3 in sky, 1 on cactus, 1 on horse blanket, 1 for sheriff's badge, 3 on blanket, 2 on boots

Lesson 2
Missing parts: bird's beak, window curtain, door, tree trunk, dog's body, wagon wheel, boy's boot, umbrella shaft

Lesson 3
Pairs of trees should match.

Lesson 4
11 triangles: 2 for owl's ears, 4 on fence posts, 1 for roof of house, 1 for witch's hat, 2 for pumpkin's eyes, 1 for pumpkin's nose

Lesson 5
Missing parts: ropes on swing, flower top, half of man's collar, man's shoe, ice-cream vendor's head, ice cream in cone, wagon wheel, girl's sock, dog's leash

Lesson 6
Pairs of kites should match.

Lesson 7
Pairs of objects should match.

Lesson 8
12 circles: 1 for sun, 1 for saucer sled, 3 for snowballs, 2 on girls' caps, 3 for snowman's body, 2 for snowman's buttons

Lesson 9
Pairs of objects should match.

Lesson 10
Missing parts: half of mustache in man's portrait, eyes and nose in woman's portrait, half of picture wire, hands on clock, numeral 3 on clock, woman's chair, candle, man's teacup, cat's head

Lesson 11
Pairs of objects should match.

Lesson 12
All *m*'s and outline of tree should be traced.

Lesson 13
Path through maze should be followed and *a*'s traced.

Lesson 14
Letters should be traced. *m*'s should be pasted near boy's mouth; *a*'s on apples.

Lesson 15
Pictures to be circled: sock, paintbrush, coin, bird

Lesson 16
Letters should be traced. *m*'s should be pasted on monkey; *a*'s by arrow.

Lesson 17
All *s*'s and outline of sailboat should be traced.

Lesson 18
Picture of a seal

Lesson 19
Pictures to be circled: pants, paper, hair, ring

Lesson 20
Path through maze should be followed and *ē*'s traced.

Lesson 21
Picture of an *ē*

Lesson 22
Pictures to be circled: necktie, plant, baseball, eating utensils

Lesson 23
Pictures to be circled: girl skating, dog chasing cat, man baking bread

Lesson 24
Path through maze should be followed and *r*'s traced.

Lesson 25
Picture of a fish

Lesson 26
Pictures to be circled: woman shivering, dirty hands, boy falling

Lesson 27
Pictures to be circled: puddle, dress, skillet, doghouse

Lesson 28
16 d's: 4 in tree, 1 on bird, 1 on tree trunk, 4 on fence, 1 by birdbath, 1 in garden, 1 in man's hand, 1 behind cat, 2 on watering can

Lesson29
Picture of a snake

Lesson 30
Pictures to be circled: ghost, hammer hitting finger, woman walking in wind, girl diving

Lesson 31
Picture of a dragon

Lesson 32
Path through maze should be followed and *f*'s traced.

Lesson 33
Picture of a bird

Lesson 34
Pictures to be circled: woman knocking over cup, baby crying, tire approaching tack, hot desert scene

Lesson 35
Picture of an insect

Lesson 36
1st row: 1, 2
2nd row: 2, 1
3rd row: 2, 1
4th row: 1, 2

Lesson 37
Picture of a bear

Lesson 38
1st row: 2, 1
2nd row: 1, 2
3rd row: 2, 1
4th row: 1, 2

Lesson 39
11 th's: 2 in picture, 1 on mantle, 1 on window, 1 on fireplace bricks, 1 in fire, 1 on top of television, 1 on television screen, 1 on chair, 1 on ottoman, 1 on rug

Lesson 40
Words should be copied.

Lesson 41
1st row: 2, 1
2nd row: 2, 1
3rd row: 1, 2
4th row: 1, 2

Lesson 42
1st row: 2, 1, 3
2nd row: 3, 2, 1
3rd row: 1, 3, 2
4th row: 2, 1, 3

Lesson 43
1st row: 2, 3, 1
2nd row: 1, 3, 2
3rd row: 3, 2, 1
4th row: 2, 1, 3

Lesson 44
Matching words should be circled.

Lesson 45
1st row: 3, 2, 1
2nd row: 2, 1, 3
3rd row: 1, 3, 2
4th row: 2, 1, 3

Lesson 46
Sequence of pictures: girl climbing slide/girl in middle of slide/girl at bottom of slide—monkey picking banana/monkey peeling banana/ monkey eating banana

Lesson 47
Words should be copied.

Lesson 48
Picture of a kangaroo

Lesson 49
Sequence of pictures: whole egg/beak poking out of egg/ chick outside of egg— man entering store/ man shopping/man leaving store

Lesson 50
A variety of sentences

Lesson 51
t pictures: toe, ten, tent, tail, tie

Lesson 52
Sequence of pictures: girl writing letter/girl putting stamp on letter/girl mailing letter—girl boarding bus/girl riding bus/girl getting off bus

Lesson 53
Phrases to be written: cat in can, ram on man, seed in sam

Lesson 54
n pictures: nest, nose, needle, nine, nail

Lesson 55
Matching words should be circled.

Lesson 56
A variety of sentences

Lesson 57
Sequence of sentences: dan is tan; dan is mad; dan is sad.

Lesson 58
c pictures: cat, cup, camel, cake, carrot

Lesson 59
Sentences should be copied.

Lesson 60
Matching words should be circled.

Lesson 61

mad	rat
sad	cat
ran	meat
fan	seat
tack	sock
sack	rock

Lesson 62
Phrases to be written: feet on dan, cat on rat, fan on fin

Lesson 63
Sentences should be copied.

Lesson 64
A variety of sentences

Lesson 65
Phrases to be written: on a cat, in a can, on a man

Lesson 66

fan	man
ram	ham
cat	can

Lesson 67
Sequence of sentences: the cat ran; the cat sat; the cat fit.

Lesson 68

ram	sun
ham	run
hit	man
sit	can
seed	tear
feed	fear

Lesson 69
Phrases to be written: a seed on sam, feed a cat, feet on a can

Lesson 70
Sentences to be circled: sam is sick; dan had a sack; he can rock; it is on a sock.

Lesson 71
h pictures: hat, horse, hand, house, hanger, ham, hose, hammer, heart

Lesson 72
Sequence of words to be pasted on: nut, name, sun, team, hot

Lesson 73
Phrases to be written: feet in mud, seed on a rug, he has a mitt

Lesson 74
Words to be written: hut, rat, rug, sun, nut, feet

Lesson 75
Sentences to be circled: it is hot; he is on a rock; mack is sad; dan has a fan.

Lesson 76
Sequence of sentences: sam is a cat; sam is a ram; sam is a man.

Lesson 77
Words to be written: cat, feet, sun, fan, hut, mud

Lesson 78
Words to be written: ant, dan, fan, ham, mitt, ram

Lesson 79
Sequence of words to be pasted on: mud, meat, feet, fit, rock

Lesson 80
Words to be circled: sad, hat, man, mud, ham

Lesson 81
A variety of sentences

Lesson 82
Matching words should be circled.

Lesson 83
Phrases to be written: ant on a mitt, fan in a hand, land on a hat

Lesson 84
Missing parts: cat's body, man's feet, girl holding umbrella, rock that boy is sitting on

Lesson 85
Words to be written: fin, man, hat, hand, sand, sun

Lesson 86
w pictures: wagon, well, windmill, witch, window

Lesson 87
Sentences to be circled: she has mail; the sock is his; it is on a hat; ron is in the mud.

Lesson 88

mitt	hut
sun	hand
man	nut

Lesson 89
Sequence of sentences: she has a fan; she has a cat; she has a rug.

Lesson 90
sh pictures: shower, shoe, sheep, shirt, shovel, shoulder, shave, ship

Lesson 91
Words to be written: lid, dish, can, ham, nut, man

Lesson 92
Phrases to be written: a cat in sand, hut on a hill, nut in a hand

Lesson 93
Missing parts: cat's ears; hut on the hill; fish on the line; ant's dish

Lesson 94

fin	lock
win	sock
nut	rock
hut	sack
sand	back
hand	shack

Lesson 95
Sequence of sentences: it has a lid; he has a hat; she has a mitt.

Lesson 96
Sentences to be circled: she hears a cow; a man has ears; she got a rug; a man has a cat.

Lesson 97
Matching words should be circled.

Lesson 98
Sentences to be written: sam is sad; dan has a hut; the ram is fat; the sun is hot.

Lesson 99
Missing parts: man's hat, shack near lake, cat on gate, man that cow is licking

Lesson 100

hate	kick
gate	sick
wish	lick
dish	sail
kiss	tail
miss	nail

Lesson 101
Sequence of sentences: a rat is not fat; a ram is fat; a cat is fat.

Lesson 102
k pictures: kite, kiss, key, kick, king

Lesson 103
Words to be circled: fish, nail, dish, read, gate, seat

Lesson 104

fin	did	ham
man	rag	nut
hat		

Lesson 105
Sentences to be written: the man is old; the cow is fat; the hat was sold; the man is mad.

Lesson 106
Missing parts: fish in lake, ant on boy's nose, cake on plate, hats on shelf

Lesson 107

sit	nut
hit	hut
sack	man
tack	can
tail	sock
mail	lock

Lesson 108
Words to be written: cow, fan, hug, mom, hat, sun

Lesson 109
(1) no *(2)* yes *(3)* yes *(4)* yes
(5) no *(6)* no *(7)* no *(8)* yes
(9) yes

Lesson 110

win	sun	hug
nod	fan	wish
cow		

Lesson 111
Sentences to be written: mom is a cop; she has a dog; dan sits in sand; he digs for fun.

Lesson 112
Sequence of words to be pasted on: cats, sail, tail, ears, cake

Lesson 113

hug	log
rug	dog
hot	goat
pot	coat
feed	seat
seed	meat

Lesson 114
Sentences to be circled: she ate a fish; this dog is sad; kick the can; we have a goat.

Lesson 115

fun	lid	sin
mud	ran	hut
mom		

Lesson 116
Sequence of sentences: see the top go; see the ship go; see the dog go.

Lesson 117
Missing parts: car under kitten, ship's sail, cop's sock, girl holding goat

Lesson 118
p pictures: pan, pie, puppet, piano, pig, pumpkin, pillow, pipe, pencil

Lesson 119

fish	kick
dish	lick
shave	sick
wave	mop
hug	cop
rug	top

Lesson 120
(1) yes *(2)* yes *(3)* no *(4)* no
(5) yes *(6)* yes *(7)* no *(8)* yes
(9) yes

Lesson 121
Sequence of words to be pasted on: oats, game, read, little, far

Lesson 122
(1) cows *(2)* top *(3)* runs *(4)* nuts
(5) feet

Lesson 123
ch pictures: chair, church, cherries, chicks, chimney, cheese, chin, chain

Lesson 124
Sentences to be written: sal has a mop; she is with sam; I hug the cat; dan wins the mitt.

Lesson 125
Sequence of words to be pasted on: chips, nose, road, wet, lake

Lesson 126
Words to be written: hats, kitten, mop, dog, teeth, kiss

Lesson 127
(1) yes *(2)* yes *(3)* no *(4)* no
(5) yes *(6)* no *(7)* no *(8)* yes
(9) no

Lesson 128
(1) hut *(2)* hill *(3)* old *(4)* red

Lesson 129
Phrases to be circled: pet in bed, ten on can, men on ship

Lesson 130
Sequence of sentences: the pot is hot; the log is hot; the sun is hot.

Lesson 131
b pictures: bicycle, ball, bus, bone, bear, belt, butterfly, banana, bed, boots, bell

Lesson 132
(1) hats *(2)* digs *(3)* girl *(4)* lid
(5) hill

Lesson 133
(1) yes *(2)* yes *(3)* no *(4)* yes
(5) yes *(6)* no *(7)* yes *(8)* yes
(9) no

Lesson 134
Words to be written: sit, boy, ship, dig, sleep, corn

Lesson 135
(1) man *(2)* cat *(3)* bed *(4)* rug

Lesson 136

arm	cow
teeth	fish
corn	feet

Lesson 137
Words to be written: waving, bug, hill, car, pot, top

Lesson 138
Phrases to be circled: cops in corn, ram hugs sam, dish on fish

Lesson 139
(1) yes *(2)* no *(3)* yes *(4)* no
(5) yes *(6)* no

Lesson 140
(1) beds *(2)* red *(3)* hand *(4)* farms
(5) ponds

Lesson 141
Words to be written: pig, cow, rabbit, boy, girl, sheep

Lesson 142
(1) pigs *(2)* farm *(3)* mud *(4)* corn

Lesson 143
Sequence of faces: mean face, sad face, happy face, sick face

Lesson 144
(1) corn *(2)* frog *(3)* barn *(4)* rugs *(5)* wins

Lesson 145
(1) no *(2)* yes *(3)* yes *(4)* no *(5)* no

Lesson 146
Sentences to be written: a girl is digging; the boy is cold; he is her brother; they see a rabbit.

Lesson 147

girl	pig
deer	dish
ship	brush

Lesson 148
(1) man with paint can *(2)* dog with bone *(3)* girl with books *(4)* girl on crutches *(5)* boy with shopping cart

Lesson 149
(1) yes *(2)* no *(3)* no *(4)* yes *(5)* no *(6)* no *(7)* no *(8)* yes *(9)* yes

Lesson 150
(1) girl *(2)* brother *(3)* bus *(4)* park

Lesson 151

red	log	box
pig	cop	old
bug		

Lesson 152
Sequence of faces: angry face, tired face, sad face, happy face

Lesson 153
Words to be written: box, broom, moon, pool, fox, room

Lesson 154
(1) cars *(2)* dark *(3)* bugs *(4)* jumps *(5)* pets

Lesson 155
(1) digging *(2)* yard *(3)* dig *(4)* fun

Lesson 156
(1) girl with fishing pole *(2)* woman in bathing suit *(3)* person in space suit *(4)* boy with cat *(5)* cow

Lesson 157
g pictures: girl, goat, gun, gate, garage, gum, guitar, ghost

Lesson 158
(1) no *(2)* yes *(3)* yes *(4)* no *(5)* yes

Lesson 159
Words to be written: well, swim, log, wet, hot, walk

Lesson 160
Sequence of faces: angry face, perspiring face, frightened face, smiling face

Fast Cycle/Reading Mastery I
Lesson Conversion Chart

Fast Cycle I is an accelerated version of *Reading Mastery I.* It is designed for students who need less repetition and drill than is provided in *Reading Mastery I,* and who can work at a faster pace.

Listed below are the *Fast Cycle/Reading Mastery I* lesson equivalents. Students at a particular lesson in the *Fast Cycle* program should be able to complete any of the worksheets in the equivalent *Reading Mastery I* lesson range.

Fast Cycle Lesson	Reading Mastery I Lesson Range	Fast Cycle Lesson	Reading Mastery I Lesson Range	Fast Cycle Lesson	Reading Mastery I Lesson Range
1	1-12	31	65-66	61	121-122
2	13-14	32	67	62	123-125
3	15-16	33	68-69	63	126
4	17-19	34	70-71	64	127-128
5	20-22	35	72-73	65	129-130
6	23	36	74-75	66	131-132
7	24-25	37	76	67	133-135
8	26	38	77-78	68	136-137
9	27	39	79-80	69	138
10	28-29	40	81-82	70	139-140
11	30-31	41	83-84	71	141-142
12	32-33	42	85-86	72	143-145
13	34-35	43	87-90	73	146
14	36	44	91	74	147
15	37-38	45	92-93	75	148-150
16	39	46	94	76	151-152
17	40-41	47	95-96	77	153-155
18	42	48	97-98	78	156
19	43-44	49	99-100	79	157
20	45	50	101-102	80	158
21	46-48	51	103-104		
22	49-50	52	105		
23	51	53	106		
24	52-54	54	107-108		
25	55-56	55	109-110		
26	57-58	56	11-112		
27	59-60	57	113-115		
28	61	58	116		
29	62-63	59	117-118		
30	64	60	119-120		